WALKING
with
LINCOLN

WALKING
with
LINCOLN

*Spiritual Strength
from America's Favorite President*

Thomas Freiling

R
Revell

a division of Baker Publishing Group
Grand Rapids, Michigan

Published by Revell
a division of Baker Publishing Group
P.O. Box 6287, Grand Rapids, MI 49516-6287
www.revellbooks.com

Printed in the United States of America

Library of Congress Cataloging-in-Publication Data
Freiling, Tom.
    Walking with Lincoln : spiritual strength from America's favorite president / Thomas Freiling.
        p.   cm.
    Includes bibliographical references.
    ISBN 978-0-8007-1901-2 (cloth)
        1. Lincoln, Abraham, 1809–1865—Religion. 2. Spiritual life. 3. Conduct of life. I. Title.
    E457.2.F788 2009
    973.7092—dc22   2008054242

Contents

CONTENTS

PREFACE

Meet the soul of Abraham Lincoln.

The sixteenth president of the United States was a deeply spiritual man, and by exploring the divine principles that guided him, you can live a more fulfilling life. Are you searching for purpose? Are you overwhelmed with trials and tragedy? Do you find yourself in the midst of a great struggle? Come walk with Lincoln, and let him show you the way.

My walk with Lincoln was, in the beginning, a heart-rending journey. Many know that Lincoln lost many loves and that he was no stranger to grief. When he was a young boy, both his mother and a sister died. As a young man, he lost his fiancée; later, as a father, he lost two sons. These losses stalked his melancholy spirit. Walt Whitman, who spent many hours with Lincoln during his presidency, said that he had a "deep latent sadness" in his expression.

I experienced a similar grief. On September 4, 2000, my wife—the mother of our two little boys—slipped away from us. I adored Deanna. "Tom, next to my Savior, you've always meant the most to me," she wrote to me in a letter shortly before dying. After a brave fight against cancer, she was gone.

Losing Deanna was a crushing blow. If you've experienced the thrill of falling in love and building a home together, you know that this can be a magical time. But our enchantment turned into dread. Deanna's loss left a gaping void in our hearts—and in our home. The absence of their mom was, of course, devastating to my sons. The house grew quiet, and the joys of home life abated. I felt rudderless.

Time passes slowly when you grieve. My long evenings turned into long nights. I'd toss and turn, and pray. I prayed that my sons would experience joy once again.

I turned to books to lighten the load of my grief. One night I grabbed William Herndon's classic 1889 biography, *Herndon's Lincoln: The True Story of a Great Life.* This book by Lincoln's former law partner was filled with interesting Lincoln lore. Having once worked for the United States Congress, I had particular interest in Lincoln's days in the nation's capital. It was a fascinating book and helped pass the time.

As I perused the pages of this old book, I stumbled across another conversation between Herndon and Lincoln, as reported by Ward Hill Lamon, Lincoln's personal bodyguard. Lincoln was not prone to discussing his childhood, but in a rare transparent moment he told Herndon, "All that I am, or hope to be, I owe to my angel mother." It struck me that Lincoln looked at the death of his mother not as a hindrance but as a help. He treasured her memory and counted it not for loss, but for hope. "I remember her prayers. They have always followed me," he said. "They have clung to me all of my life." The loss didn't ruin young Abe! This broken little boy rose to greatness.

It might not seem like much, but I was comforted by this morsel of Lincoln's story. It was a signpost on my way out of grief. Abraham Lincoln, a man of great sorrow who endured trials and tribulations through his entire life, mustered the strength to overcome his frailties and weaknesses. He was battered but not beaten. This was an example for me and my sons to live by. I don't know if my prayers caused me to read this story, but I thanked God for it.

This is how I began my walk with Lincoln. It gave me hope in my future; and, in Lincoln's words, "The power of hope upon human exertion is wonderful."

The more I learned about Lincoln, the more I marveled at the strength of his endurance. His lot in life was hard, even by eighteenth-century backwoods standards. But he seemed resilient beyond measure. He rose from disgrace to distinction. Yet no self-help books were available for him to read. Therapists and antidepressants didn't exist, and he couldn't lean on Oprah or Dr. Phil for help. The nearest church from his boyhood home was a half-day's walk away. He was, literally, on his own.

Or was he?

What was his prescription for successful living? What guided Lincoln through the turmoil and ill-fated circumstances? Where did his inner strength come from?

Famed philosopher Reinhold Niebuhr—author of the Serenity Prayer—studied the life of Lincoln and concluded that his "religious convictions were superior in depth and purity to those, not only of political leaders of his day, but of religious leaders of the era."

Indeed, if you read much about Lincoln, you can't help but notice how prominent a role religion played in his life.

So I decided to become a student of Lincoln's faith. I searched for books and articles about his religious convictions. Surprisingly, my initial efforts yielded nothing. Plenty of books have been written about Lincoln's political prowess, his ideology, or his skills as commander in chief. But recent historians have all but ignored Lincoln's faith. It seems that when contemporary scholars explore the inner Abraham Lincoln, they focus on his feelings, his psyche, or even his sexuality—but not his faith. This is a shame because even a cursory look at Lincoln's life and words reveals that he was intensely spiritual.

For example, Doris Kearns Goodwin's bestselling *Team of Rivals* makes little mention of Lincoln's faith; when it does, her descriptions are superficial and restricted to direct quotes from Lincoln.

Eventually my search transported me back decades, even a century. I combed rare-book shops, searched the Internet, and visited archives at the Abraham Lincoln Presidential Library in Springfield, Illinois. In the end, I discovered a mountain of material pertaining to Lincoln's faith. It's hard to fathom why this topic has gone unnoticed for so long.

The first book I devoured was William Barton's *The Soul of Abraham Lincoln*, written in 1920. In his outstanding study of

Lincoln's spirituality, Barton thoroughly examined the topic and accumulated an enormous collection of materials. I reviewed these documents at the University of Chicago, where they are now held.

Other similar studies were written from 1900 to the late 1960s. For example, in 1948, Edgar DeWitt Jones penned *Lincoln and the Preachers*, in which he fastidiously documented Lincoln's conversations with ministers and theologians of his era. William J. Wolf, a theology professor at Union Theological Seminary, published a study of Lincoln's religious beliefs in 1959 entitled *The Almost Chosen People*. During the same era, prominent Presbyterian minister Clarence Macartney wrote a primer entitled *Lincoln and the Bible*, while Harlan Hoyt Horner's *The Growth of Lincoln's Faith* became a bestseller. I also traced my steps back to early memoirists like Francis Carpenter, who spent six months inside Lincoln's White House. Carpenter penned his observations in the first Lincoln biography, published in 1866. Later that year Josiah Holland, a Puritan and editor of the *Springfield Republican*, wrote the first thoroughly researched Lincoln epic, entitled *The Life of Abraham Lincoln*. That same year, Isaac Arnold, an abolitionist and friend of Lincoln, wrote *A History of Abraham Lincoln*; later John Wesley Hill, who accompanied Lincoln on campaign stops in Illinois, wrote *Abraham Lincoln: Man of God*. Each of these studies and biographies addresses Lincoln's faith and spirituality directly. They don't skirt the issue; they embrace it. Although each one provides a somewhat different perspective, similar themes begin to emerge.

For example, Lincoln revered Scripture as the "perfect moral code." He said the Bible spoke to people "in all conditions of life." It contained "all things most desirable for man's welfare," and he doused speeches and letters with biblical references and allusions. The Second Inaugural Address was so peppered with New Testament references that Wolf called it "one of the most astute pieces of Christian theology ever written." Lincoln committed much of the Bible to memory and possessed a remarkable ability to apply its teachings in everyday situations. Carl Sandburg said he knew the Bible "from cover to cover."

Other spiritual themes prominent in Lincoln's life and words include the importance of prayer and trust in God; a belief in providence and destiny; and a strong commitment to morality, self-control, mercy, justice, and love of neighbor. He believed that the will of God was knowable. He displayed deep compassion and humility, and despite his melancholy nature he learned how to take pleasure in simple things.

As I sorted through these and other themes, I learned a great deal—and I began to apply his lessons to my life. Lincoln's spiritual principles are as applicable today as they were during the Civil War. A "perpetual freshness is found in the words of Lincoln," wrote Archer Shaw, author of *The Lincoln Encyclopedia*. They possess an "indestructible quality."

In this book I give you the soul of Lincoln in fifty faith-filled readings based on his life and words. These are not pious tales. Thanks to the painstaking work of historians who sifted the facts from fiction, I give you the bona fide "honest Abe."

I hope this book encourages you and nudges you to nurture your spiritual growth. I make no political arguments in this book, and I try not to proselytize. Lincoln was a uniter, not a divider. He never joined a church, and he refused to endorse any particular Christian dogma. He told Connecticut congressman Henry C. Deming, "When any church will inscribe over its altar as the sole qualification for membership the Savior's condensed statement of the substance of both law and gospel: 'Thou shalt love the Lord thy God with all thy heart and with all thy soul and with all thy mind, and love thy neighbor as thyself,' that church will I join with all my heart." That's the magnetism of Lincoln's faith. It transcends the trivialities that divide us.

Some of these stories may be familiar. Others may surprise you. Most of them point without hesitation or embarrassment to the Bible. Make no mistake: this is not trendy self-help spirituality. Lincoln's faith was rooted deeply in the truths found in the Old and New Testaments of the Holy Bible. They are truths so simple that we tend to overlook them. Some people may call them old-fashioned; I like to think of them as timeless. They worked for Lincoln. They can work for you.

On a cold winter night in 1862, Lincoln's secretary found him pacing the floor. He'd been awake all night. The Union armies had just been devastated, losing 26,000 soldiers in Fredericksburg, Virginia. Thousands of wives and mothers mourned. The president was anguished; his eyes were said to be "deathly." He paced back and forth, asking himself over and over, "What has God put me in this place for?"

Are you asking yourself a similar question, "Why, God?"

Come walk with Lincoln and discover how to pass through your fiery trials on your way to victory.

I would be remiss not to mention Melissa Killian, my editor, for her assistance in taking my sometimes jumbled and scattered thoughts into what you read here. Melissa is a true professional, and her dedication to this project cannot be underestimated. I also want to thank Andrea Doering and the entire staff at Revell for their valuable contributions to this book. What a team!

When I showed the original manuscript to friends and family, they demanded that I finish the story of what happened to my family and our home—the "happily ever after" part. Just as Thomas Lincoln (Abe's father) found Sarah Bush, I met and married a beautiful and devoted woman—a new mother for my sons. Nancy mended our home and taught us how to laugh again. Best of all, she instilled in us the same kinds of values that Sarah taught young Abe. I dedicate this book to her. Thank you, Nancy.

1

Fear Not

We live in the midst of alarms; anxiety beclouds our future; we expect some new disaster with each newspaper we read.

Abraham Lincoln

Abraham Lincoln certainly had reason to worry and to be afraid. But not unlike the patriarchs in the Old Testament, who were required to fight wars against impossible odds, evade plots against their lives, and cope with overwhelming grief, Lincoln found the peace that only comes from God. President Lincoln must have understood King David's feelings, not only in facing daunting adversity, but also in his unwavering reliance on God's grace and faithfulness.

Lincoln once visited with one of his generals after his near-execution by a twelve-pound cannonball at Gettysburg. Major General Sickles asked Lincoln if he was anxious about the Battle of Gettysburg, where more than fifty thousand Union and Confederate soldiers died. Lincoln replied that he was not. When the general inquired how this could be, Lincoln hesitated before giving the following explanation:

> Well, I will tell you how it was. In the pinch of your campaign up there, when everybody seemed panic-stricken, and nobody could tell what was going to happen, oppressed by the gravity of our affairs, I went to my room one day, and I locked the door, and got down on my knees before Almighty God, and prayed to Him mightily for victory at Gettysburg. I told Him that this was His war, and our cause His cause. . . . And I then and there made a solemn vow to Almighty God, that if He would stand by our boys at Gettysburg, I would stand by Him.

God honored Lincoln's prayer, and Lincoln honored his promise. Lincoln explained to the general that soon after he prayed, "a sweet comfort crept into my soul that God Almighty had taken the whole business into his own hands and that things would go all right at Gettysburg. And that is why I had no fears about you." Indeed, the Battle of Gettysburg was the turning point for the Union army in the Civil War.

Neither was Lincoln afraid for his own life, even though he was repeatedly warned about the plots against him. During the Civil War a prominent Presbyterian minister, Charles Chiniquy, visited Lincoln on several occasions to caution him about the impending danger of assassination. To these warnings Lincoln replied: "I see no other safeguard against these murderers, but to be always ready to die, as Christ advises it. As we must all die sooner or later, it makes very little difference to me whether I die from a dagger plunged through the heart or from an inflammation of the lungs."

There's nothing new about fear and anxiety, although it's tempting to believe that people today are more stressed and afraid than at any time in history. News reports barrage us with messages declaring that all is wrong in the world—rumors of war, epidemics, political unrest, stock market volatility, and the breakdown of the family. It's enough to drive us into a state of panic, and many people today suffer from depression and anxiety. But worry isn't a new phenomenon. Jesus warned us that we would have problems in this world, and he gave us the power to overcome our worries.

Lincoln relied on the Bible's answer to overcoming fear and anxiety. He opened his Bible in the presence of Father Chiniquy and read from Deuteronomy 3:23–25:

> Then I pleaded with the LORD at that time, saying: "O Lord GOD, You have begun to show Your servant Your greatness and Your mighty hand, for what god is there in heaven or on earth who can do anything like Your works and Your mighty deeds? I pray, let me cross over and see the good land beyond the Jordan, those pleasant mountains, and Lebanon."

The Lord answered Moses that only with his eyes would he see the land of promise; because of the sins of the people, he would not enter into it. Lincoln felt convinced that those passages of Scripture were also meant for him. After reading them aloud he added with the gravest sincerity, "Just as the Lord heard no murmur from the lips of Moses when He told him that he had to die before crossing the Jordan for the sins of his people, so I hope and pray that He will hear no murmur from me when I fall for my nation's sake."

Lincoln understood that only by laying down his life could he find it. He also knew that only in God's presence could one find the peace needed to overcome the overwhelming sense of fear and distress that often comes from living in a war-torn world. Like King David and Moses before him, he did not rely on his own understanding, but put his complete trust in God.

> You will keep him in perfect peace,
> Whose mind is stayed on You,
> Because he trusts in You.
>
> Isaiah 26:3

2

ASK FOR PRAYER

I have been driven many times to my knees by the over-whelming conviction that I had nowhere else to go.

Abraham Lincoln

As Moses departed from Mount Sinai to lead the Israelites into the Promised Land, he told God, "If Your Presence does not go with us, do not bring us up from here" (Exod. 33:15). Moses recognized that a difficult and complicated job lay ahead of him. He wouldn't succeed except with God's help. He'd rather be a faith-filled desert wanderer than a godless freedom fighter.

Lincoln faced a similar challenge. His victory in the election of 1860 hinged on the issue of slavery. During the campaign

21

he asked, "Can we as Christian men, strong and free ourselves, wield the sledge or hold the iron which is to manacle anew an already oppressed race?" But secessionist clamor in the South grew, and rumors reverberated that Jefferson Davis would soon become provisional president of a new Confederate States of America.

Lincoln bore a heavy burden, and his friends say his demeanor changed after being elected president—even before leaving for Washington, DC. Solemn and resolute, he boarded the train leaving his home in Springfield, Illinois. Journalists were told that he would make no public comments. But as a throng of people gathered, Lincoln felt compelled to address them. He scribbled notes on a scrap of paper and walked to the back of the train. Removing his hat, he paused and looked at the crowd. The lively crowd fell silent, and every man removed his hat. All eyes focused on Lincoln as he glanced down at his notes. He breathed deeply in an effort to control his emotions and spoke briefly.

> I now leave, not knowing when, or whether ever, I may return, with a task before me greater than that which rested upon George Washington. Washington never would have succeeded except for the aid of Divine Providence, upon which all times he relied. I feel that I cannot succeed without the same Divine aid which sustained him, and on the same Almighty Being I place my reliance and support.

As he concluded, emotions ran high. *New York Herald* reporter Henry Villard wrote that many in the audience were moved to tears. Some were taken aback by Lincoln's next request: "I hope you, my friends, will all pray that I receive Divine assistance." As the train pulled away, many ran after it crying out, "We will pray for you, Mr. Lincoln!" The women and girls waved their handkerchiefs and threw flowers at the caboose. The next time the people of Springfield gathered on his behalf, they hosted his funeral.

At stops along the 1,094 miles to Washington, DC—through Indiana, Ohio, and Pennsylvania, up to New York and down through Trenton and Philadelphia—Lincoln stepped to the back of the train and called on God's name. "Without the assistance of that Supreme Being who has never forsaken us I shall surely fail," he said in Buffalo. "With my own ability I cannot succeed, with the sustenance of Divine Providence, I cannot fail," he proclaimed in Newark. Over and over, he asked for prayer.

Lincoln's plea serves as a good model for us. It's not a sign of doubt or faithlessness to admit that we will "surely fail" without God's assistance. On the contrary, when we rely on God, we admit that relying on our own strength will only lead to frustration and confusion. Lincoln forfeited his pride and freely admitted he was not up to the task ahead of him without God's divine enablement.

If you have a big undertaking ahead of you, solicit the prayers of the people around you. Don't be ashamed to admit you aren't up to the task. Lincoln cautioned, "Intoxicated by unbroken success, we have become too self-sufficient to feel the necessity of redeeming and preserving grace, too proud to pray to the God that made us." Your weakness is made perfect in God's strength. Ask for prayer.

The LORD your God in your midst,
The Mighty One, will save;
He will rejoice over you with gladness,
He will quiet you with His love.

Zephaniah 3:17

3

Practice Humility

What kills a skunk is the publicity it gives itself.

Abraham Lincoln

Contrary to popular belief, the Bible does not say, "God helps those who help themselves." Self-promotion might be a common strategy in today's world, but it isn't the secret to success in a God-empowered life. Instead, God gives grace to the humble, not to the proud and self-important.

Abraham Lincoln exuded humility and conducted himself with a self-effacing demeanor. Lincoln was unpretentious; worked hard; studied diligently; and, according to his law partner John Todd Stuart, "made friends everywhere he went." He never envisioned for himself the role of emancipator. "I am not an accomplished lawyer," Lincoln once professed, despite having built a successful practice without a law degree. "I am not a professional lecturer," he claimed after making a speech that was met with rousing applause. Lincoln made less of himself, not more, and was noticeably modest. "In my life I have seen a good number of men distinguished by their talents," wrote journalist Edward Dicey, "but I never saw anyone, so apparently unconscious that this distinction conferred upon him any superiority as Abraham Lincoln."

Make no mistake, Lincoln was ambitious and driven, but these traits were subject to his modesty. He said, "I must in candor say I do not think myself fit for the Presidency, but I certainly am flattered and gratified that some partial friends think of me in that connection."

Lincoln initially laughed at attempts by friends to suggest that he run for president. He didn't even attend the 1860 Republican Convention—the same convention at which he was surprisingly nominated. "You would perhaps be only preparing a disappointment for yourselves," he told followers, "and as a consequence of your disappointment, mortification for me." Even so, his admirers managed to get his name on the ballot. "He is one of the best men God ever made," said a supporter.

By all standards, Lincoln lacked image. Before being elected president, he served only a single term in Congress—hardly a legislative legacy. He held no high-level appointments, never won a statewide victory, and had no previous executive experience whatsoever (unless you count his days as postmaster in New Salem). Aside from a six-month stint as an anti-slavery lecturer throughout the Midwest and Northeast, Lincoln had neither a distinguished résumé nor an impressive list of accomplishments.

And as a candidate, Lincoln was anything but ostentatious. Amazingly, he made only one public appearance during the presidential campaign. "It has been my purpose, since I have been *placed* in this position, to make no speeches," he said plainly from his home in Springfield. When newspapers tried to inject excitement into the race, he bluntly remarked, "It is a great folly to attempt to make anything out of me or my early life." Meanwhile, his opponent, Stephen A. Douglas, fought tenaciously. Douglas towered over Lincoln in fame and credentials. He patronized Lincoln, calling him "kind and amiable, but totally inapprehensive." A stalwart partisan and the most powerful legislator in Washington, Douglas had already run for president twice, barely losing contests to Franklin Pierce and James Buchanan. He was known as the "little giant" for his sarcastic and scathing style.

But on November 6, 1860, voters dismissed Douglas's style for what Phineas Gurley, chaplain of the United States Senate, called Lincoln's "calm and abiding confidence in the overruling providence of God." Voters swarmed the polls in record numbers (eight of ten Americans voted) and handed Lincoln a stunning victory. Lincoln won 180 electoral votes to 12 for Senator Douglas. William Lee Miller suggested, "It can be said that by the formal test of offices held and great deeds accomplished, he was the least qualified man ever elected, perhaps ever nominated by either party."

Neighbors in Springfield were flabbergasted. To them, he was a country lawyer who spent as much time hauling his sons up and down the street in a little wagon as he did litigating. Springfield gossip even went so far as to call him henpecked. One astonished neighbor reportedly asked, "Abe Lincoln for President of the United States? Can it be possible? A man that buys a ten-cent stamp beefsteak for breakfast, and carries it home himself!"

True humility is not lazy or self-despising; instead, it is seeing ourselves as God and others see us. Lincoln unwittingly unlocked the door to true greatness through humility. Like David in the Old Testament who served in the court of tempestuous King Saul, Lincoln served faithfully in the small things. He didn't bluster his way to the top, and when he was asked to lead, he responded like David, "Who am I, O Lord GOD?" (2 Sam. 7:18).

> For by the grace given me I say to every one of you: Do not think of yourself more highly than you ought, but rather think of yourself with sober judgment, in accordance with the measure of faith God has given you.
>
> Romans 12:3 NIV

4

GO TO GOD'S WORD

*In regard to this Great Book, I have but to say, it is
the best gift God has given to man. All the good the
Savior gave to the world was communicated through
this book.*

Abraham Lincoln

*L*incoln referred to the Bible almost habitually, both
in public addresses and in private conversation. "If a
public man were to quote the Bible today as frequently as Lincoln did during the Civil War," observed Clarence Macartney
in 1908, "he would be charged with cant or hypocrisy."

Do you go to the Bible routinely or only as a last resort?
Sometimes we fail to rely on God's Word, depending instead

on our knowledge or a book or magazine for help. But Lincoln relied on the Bible as a first option.

Without question, Lincoln knew the Bible better than any other American president. But this was not always true. For a time Lincoln doubted, even scoffed at the Bible. Early in his political career, he fashioned himself as a successful, self-made man. He held the Bible at bay in order to take on more "intellectual pursuits." He studied Thomas Paine and the French atheist philosopher C. F. Volney. He regarded the Bible as passé and its lessons as too ancient for modern application. He sparred with local ministers, and local townspeople dubbed him a "heathen." He allegedly penned a book, long since lost, denying the veracity of Scripture.

During this time, Lincoln's stature also began to rise. A self-taught lawyer and rising politico, he ran successfully for the Illinois state legislature. The naive backwoods boy had grown into a more sophisticated and ambitious young man.

But Lincoln's star didn't shine for long. His pride soon turned to shame. In 1835 his first love, Ann Rutledge, died. Six years later at age 32, he was still unwed and involved in an on-again, off-again love affair with Mary Todd. His law practice faltered, he sank into debt, and a string of legislative deals under his leadership left the Illinois economy in shambles. His nerves were in shambles as well. He was a "no show" during important sessions of the legislature, and he drifted aimlessly around town in the middle of the night. The *New Salem Register* even sneered at his excessively nervous "indisposition." Finally Lincoln crashed. Nearly suicidal, he was confined to bed rest under the care of a doctor.

A friend named Joshua Speed pulled Lincoln out of his deep, dark hole. They often rode to the general store together, and Speed's large family developed a fondness for Lincoln. One morning Speed's mother, Lucy Gilmer, visited Lincoln to encourage him. She quoted passages of Scripture to put him at ease and gave him an Oxford edition of the Bible.

The incident, later recorded by Speed, was a defining moment for Lincoln. "Tell your mother," Lincoln wrote to Speed, "I have not got her present with me, but that I intend to read it regularly when I return home. I doubt not that it really is, as she says, the best cure for the blues."

Many years later Speed reminisced that Lincoln then "sought to make the Bible a preceptor to his faith and a guide to his conduct." Speed reported that he once found Lincoln sitting near a window in the White House, immersed in the Bible. Lincoln admonished him, "Take all of this [the Bible] upon reason that you can, and the balance on faith, and you will live and die a happier and better man."

Congressman Adlai E. Stevenson, who later served as vice president under Grover Cleveland, observed the way Lincoln used Bible stories as analogies when they discussed the war effort. Speaking to L. E. Chittenden, the register of the treasury, Lincoln said, "I decided a long time ago that it was less difficult to believe that the Bible was what it claimed to be, than to disbelieve it." Lincoln's son Robert recalled that, "in the later years of his life, he always had a Bible very near him," and it comforted him "at all times."

Do you rely on the Bible, or do you question its relevancy? It's natural to wrestle with doubts. "Those days of trouble found me tossed amidst a sea of questionings," Lincoln confessed. But he learned an important lesson. He couldn't find his way until he rediscovered God's Word. "The Scriptures unfolded before me with deeper and more logical appeal than anything else I could find to turn to, or ever before I had found in them."

We may have traded horses for cars and letters for emails, but problems remain the same. We face similar challenges in our world, our marriages, our families, and our work. We can go our own way, or like Lincoln, rely on the Bible and die "happier and better" for it.

> By your words I can see where I'm going;
>> they throw a beam of light on my dark path. . . .
> Everything's falling apart on me, God;
>> put me together again with your Word.
> Festoon me with your finest sayings, God;
>> teach me your holy rules. . . .
> I inherited your book on living; it's mine forever—
>> what a gift! And how happy it makes me!

> Psalm 119:105–112
> Message

5

LAUGH AT YOUR PROBLEMS

*With the fearful strain that is on me night and day, if
I did not laugh I should die.*

Abraham Lincoln

*I*magine Abraham Lincoln sitting on a box of dry goods
with both feet firmly planted on the floor, much like his
statue sits in the Lincoln Memorial. Imagine him engaging
his listeners with his wisdom and eloquence. He is telling a
story. As he speaks, his eyes twinkle; he lifts one foot off the
floor and motions with his hands; finally, as the story reaches
its height, he throws back his head in unrestrained laughter
as he delivers the punch line. "Every one present willing or

unwilling were compelled to take part," remarked a colleague of one such occasion.

For Lincoln, happiness was a choice. Despite his difficult circumstances and the stress that accompanies being a leader, he chose to laugh. We, too, can choose to be glum or choose to be droll. Neither response will change our circumstances, but our choice will change the way we believe and behave.

Lincoln developed the art—and habit—of humor to lift himself out of his otherwise perpetual melancholy. Lincoln's law partner William Herndon described how Lincoln withdrew into spells of depression only to gather his wits by saying, "Billy, that reminds me of a story." Herndon tells how Lincoln would "walk up and down the room laughing the while and how the dark clouds would pass off his withered and wrinkled face."

Humor distracted Lincoln and brought relief from the mental storms that continuously hovered on the horizons of his mind. It's a lesson we need to learn over and over again. "A good story," he said, "has the same effect on me that I think a good square drink of whisky has to the old roper. It puts new life into me . . . good for both the mental and physical digestion." He also remarked that "if it were not for these stories—jokes—jests I should die; they give vent—are the vents of my moods and gloom."

If nothing else, Lincoln was remarkably self-aware and honest with his feelings. He was as authentic as he was transparent. A fellow lawyer, Clark E. Carr, once wrote, "It was because Abraham Lincoln was the most human of human beings that he is loved as has never been any other man that ever lived."

Lincoln's humor brought with it a sense of hope as well as healing. Of this attribute one friend recounted:

> I have heard men say that they had laughed at his stories until they had almost shaken their ribs loose. I heard cases where men had been suffering for years from some bodily ailment and could get no relief but who have gone a couple of evenings and listened to Lincoln and laughed their ailments away, and become hale and hearty men, giving Lincoln credit of being their healer.

William Herndon once wrote of a common occurrence while traveling the Eighth Judicial Circuit with Lincoln: "In the morning we would all be sore from the excessive laughing; the judge, the lawyers, the jurymen, the witnesses and all. Our sides and back would ache all through."

Lincoln was a man not only of serious and devoted prayer, but also of spontaneous and deliberate laughter. He could stir up a joke or harness the power of mirth at will. However, not all of his peers shared Lincoln's panache. On more than one occasion he shook his fellow legislators loose from their stoic demeanor. "Gentlemen," he once urged, "why don't you laugh? If I didn't laugh under the strain that is upon me day and night, I should go mad. And you need that medicine as well as I!"

Do you know someone who is particularly funny? Do you find yourself wanting to be around that person? We all need to laugh, whether or not we even realize it at times. We seek out laughter and look for it to put us at ease, especially during times of stress.

Humor never failed to put Lincoln, or those he met, at ease. On the campaign trail, his sense of fun and charming wit earned him favor with voters, and at the end of a long day of delivering speeches and shaking hands, he retired to a local tavern where he engaged in the "narration of a story. The tavern loungers enjoyed it, and his melancholy, taking to itself wings, seemed to fly away."

It was during such a time that a newspaper reporter overheard two Quaker women on a train engage in the following conversation:

"I think Jefferson will succeed."

"Why does thee think so?"

"Because Jefferson is a praying man."

"And so is Abraham a praying man."

"Yes, but the Lord will think Abraham is joking."

Lincoln was not merely a jokester. He was keenly aware of his own weaknesses and the shortcomings he saw around him. He understood that a "merry heart does good, like medicine" (Prov. 17:22) and that society suffered too many ills—as did he—to neglect its use. Humor was the spoonful of sugar that enabled him to convince difficult people to swallow the difficult things during difficult times. About his use of comic story, Lincoln once reflected:

The sharpness of a refusal or the edge of a rebuke may be blunted by an appropriate story, so as to save wounded feeling and yet serve the purpose. No, I am not simply a storyteller, but storytelling as an emollient saves me much friction and distress.

Humor was indeed a powerful force against the onslaught of conflict and despair. It is a powerful force we all need.

> And the voice of those who make merry;
> I will multiply them, and they shall not diminish;
> I will also glorify them, and they shall not be small.
>
> Jeremiah 30:19

6

WEIGH THE CASE FOR CHRIST

*Probably it is to be my lot to go on in twilight, feeling
and reasoning my way through life, as questioning,
doubting Thomas did. But in my poor, maimed way,
I bear with me as I go on a spirit of desire for a faith
that was with him of olden time, who, in his need, as
I in mine, exclaimed, "Help thou my unbelief."*

Abraham Lincoln

From time to time we doubt God. We become skeptics,
questioning God's purposes and sometimes even his
very existence. It's natural to feel some misgivings, especially
when we experience difficult times in our lives. But when our
hearts are weak and our faith is challenged, it's a good time to
let our minds weigh the case for Christ.

Abraham Lincoln took few things for granted. As with his study of law and politics, he committed himself fully to understanding the Bible. He made no claims of knowing more than he did. And when it came to knowing what he believed and why, he approached his subject with a degree of introspection and tenacity that was remarkable for someone formerly known as a skeptic.

Interestingly, his skepticism, grief, and loss propelled him—rather than repelled him—into a season of exploration and discovery of Scripture. In 1850 Mary and Abraham's second son, Eddie, died of what was likely diphtheria, just weeks before his fourth birthday. The rector of the Episcopal church they had been attending was out of town, so the funeral was conducted at the Presbyterian church by its presiding minister, Dr. James Smith. Rev. Smith proved to be a source of great comfort to the Lincoln family, so much so that the Lincolns remained among his most faithful congregants until they left Springfield for Washington, DC.

Not long after the death of their son, the Lincolns visited Mary's relatives in her hometown of Lexington, Kentucky. While there, Mr. Lincoln came across a book entitled *The Christian Defense*, which piqued his interest. He was surprised to discover that the author of the book was Dr. Smith. Greatly intrigued by the straightforward style of Smith's apologetics, he obtained his own copy and discussed the book with Smith after he returned to Springfield. "I found him very much depressed and downcast at the death of his son and without the consolation of the gospel," recalled Smith. "I had heard . . . [that he] was inclined to skepticism as to the divine origin of the Scriptures, though, unlike most skeptics, he had been a constant reader of the Bible."

Dr. Smith had struggled with his own doubts regarding the Christian faith but after a great deal of study had come to believe that the Scriptures were indeed inspired. An avid defender of the faith, Smith wrote his book in response to the skeptics whom he often debated. He recalled how Lincoln discovered for himself the reliability of the truths laid forth in the Bible: "I found him an honest and anxious inquirer. . . . Mr. Lincoln took the book, and for a number of weeks, as a lawyer, examined and weighed the evidence, pro and con." In a letter to Lincoln's law partner William Herndon, Smith recalled:

> To the arguments on both sides Mr. Lincoln gave a most patient, impartial and searching investigation. The result was the announcement made by himself that the argument in favor of the divine authority and inspiration of the Scriptures was unanswerable.
>
> Some months later, Mr. Lincoln was invited to deliver a lecture on the Bible at the Presbyterian Church. A full house gathered to hear what the grave Mr. Lincoln would say, and [said] that he gave "the ablest defense of the Bible ever uttered in that pulpit." Although Lincoln continued to wrestle with his faith, as we all do from time to time, he continued to pursue God. But this painful period of searching provided a foothold that enabled him to step onto more solid ground.

For Lincoln, and for us, doubting is sometimes the path to knowing. When we search, we find. When we knock, the door opens. In the end, we're better believers as a result of our doubt.

> Therefore, my beloved, as you have always obeyed, not as in my presence only, but now much more in my absence, work out your own salvation with fear and trembling; for it is God who works in you both to will and to do for His good pleasure.
>
> Philippians 2:12–13

7

TRUST IN GOD

*What I did, I did after very full deliberation, and under
a heavy and solemn sense of responsibility. I can only
trust in God that I have made no mistake.*

Abraham Lincoln

Three years into the Civil War, Americans questioned
its meaning and purpose. So Lincoln called upon the
country to trust in God. "While it has not pleased the Almighty
to bless us with a return of peace, we can but press on, guided
by the best light He gives us, trusting that in His good time
and wise way all will yet be well," he exhorted the nation. He
continued to place his trust in God, and he appealed to the
country to do the same through his speeches and proclama-

tions calling for days of prayer, fasting, and thanksgiving, until the end of the war.

At the outset of his presidency, Lincoln appointed James Pollock as director of the Philadelphia Mint. Pollock had just been elected governor of Pennsylvania after serving in Congress for several years. However, Pollock was best known for his strong Christian faith. Pollock, along with Secretary of the Treasury Salmon P. Chase, recommended to Lincoln that the words "In God We Trust" be inscribed on all U.S. coins.

On March 3, 1865, Congress passed an act allowing the director of the mint—with the secretary of the treasury's approval—to place the motto on all gold and silver coins. This act, one of the last passed by Congress before Lincoln's death, immortalized the essence of his heart. "I trust through the good sense of the American people, on all sides of all rivers in America, under the providence of God, who has never deserted us, that we shall again be brethren." One nation under God—in God we still trust.

Lincoln understood that he could not trust in his own understanding. He was forced to trust in God. We must still trust in God as a nation today. Even more than ever, as wars rage across the globe, we must place our trust in the Almighty, the Creator of the universe.

> Trust in the LORD with all your heart,
> And lean not on your own understanding;
> In all your ways acknowledge Him,
> And He shall direct your paths.
>
> Proverbs 3:5–6

8

RELY ON SCRIPTURE
AS A DAILY GUIDE

*But for [the Bible] we could not know right from wrong.
All things most desirable for man's welfare, here and
hereafter, are to be found portrayed in it.*

Abraham Lincoln

The Bible offers us more than inspirational words to be read from the pulpit on Sunday morning. It's also full of sound advice for everyday living. For Lincoln, the Bible was more than a sacred scroll; it was a source of practical wisdom. He relied on it for answers to problems and issues he faced as a respected lawyer and politician. Moreover, he wasn't ashamed to say so. In a conversation with the register of the treasury,

L. E. Chittenden, Lincoln divulged his beliefs regarding the legitimacy of the Bible and its inherent value:

> The character of the Bible is easily established, at least to my satisfaction. It is a good book for us to obey—it contains the Ten Commandments, the Golden Rule, and many other rules which ought to be followed. No man was ever the worse for living according to the directions of the Bible.

His political opponents generally found themselves on dangerous ground when they attempted to quote Scripture when refuting Lincoln. For example, when Stephen A. Douglas cited Adam and Eve as the first beneficiaries of "popular sovereignty" (a doctrine that allowed settlers of new territories to determine the status of slavery for themselves), Lincoln adeptly corrected him: "God did not place good and evil before man, telling him to make his choice. On the contrary, he did tell him there was one tree, of the fruit of which he should not eat, upon pain of certain death." Then added Lincoln pointedly, "I should scarcely wish so strong a prohibition against slavery in Nebraska."

On another occasion, when Lincoln was misinformed that thousands had nominated Republican dissident John Fremont for president when only four hundred were actually present, he immediately found the number significant. Reaching for his Bible, he quickly turned to 1 Samuel 22:2 and read about David in the cave of Adullam: "And every one that was in distress, and every one that was in debt, and every one that was discontented, gathered themselves unto him; and he became captain over them: and there were with him about four hundred men" (KJV). Not only was he an impressive Bible scholar, he also managed to draw upon his knowledge of the Bible to sketch often enlightening, if not amusing, analogies.

Lincoln's Second Inaugural Address ultimately became the climactic expression of his faith. Many have insisted that it resembles a sermon more than a speech. In it he made fourteen references to God, included four direct quotations from Scripture (Gen. 3:19; Ps. 19:7–9; Matt. 7:1–3; 1 Peter 4:8), and made additional allusions to biblical teaching. The London *Spectator* commented prophetically on this Scripture-steeped masterpiece:

> We cannot read it without a renewed conviction that it is the noblest political document known to history, and should have for the nation and the statesmen he left behind him something of a sacred and almost prophetic character. Surely, none was ever written under a stronger sense of the reality of God's government. And certainly none written in a period of passionate conflict ever so completely excluded the partiality of victorious faction, and breathed so pure a strain of mingled justice and mercy.

This speech became one of Lincoln's most influential, if not commonly remembered, legacies. At a time when the nation faced its most critical crisis in history—when the very fiber of its union was threatened—the president drew timeless wisdom from the deep wells of Scripture for answers. It was also Lincoln's last public address. The following month he was assassinated.

Lincoln's deep knowledge of Scripture gave him an upper hand when he was confronted with difficult situations. He unashamedly relied on the truths—and lived by the commands—of the Bible. Likewise, we need not feel awkward about following Scripture—even in the workplace. In order to do that, though, we must commit ourselves to learning and studying the Word of God—like Lincoln. Scripture served as the plumb line which aligned the affairs of his life, and in turn it endued him with the wisdom and grace he needed to lead the country through its darkest hour—and it will give you the wisdom and grace you need to carry out your calling.

> All Scripture is given by inspiration of God, and is profitable for doctrine, for reproof, for correction, for instruction in righteousness, that the man of God may be complete, thoroughly equipped for every good work.
>
> 2 Timothy 3:16–17

9

LET THE LITTLE CHILDREN COME

Children have the first place.

Abraham Lincoln

*B*usy parents sometimes forget to put their kids before themselves. They climb career ladders, allowing the years to pass by without getting to know their children. Lincoln busied himself climbing ladders too, but after his son died, Lincoln wrote a poem entitled "Little Eddie," which the *Illinois State Journal* printed by request. It is very poignant and tender. Here is the last of the four stanzas:

> Angel Boy—fare thee well, farewell
> Sweet Eddie, We bid thee adieu!
> Affection's wail cannot reach thee now
> Deep though it be, and true.

Bright is the home to him now given
For "of such is the Kingdom of Heaven."

Lincoln echoed the words of Jesus, who told his disciples, "Let the little children come to Me, and do not forbid them; for of such is the kingdom of heaven" (Matt. 19:14). No doubt he loved children and saw in them something heavenly.

Whether Lincoln's fondness for children stemmed from the loss of two of his own, or from his own wretchedly painful childhood, or because he understood "for of such is the kingdom of heaven," he was no doubt a doting father and willing participant in many a youthful game. As president, he relished the company of his boys in his office; as a houseguest, he enjoyed engaging the youngsters in raucous games. On one such occasion, it was noted that his "coat tails sailed out behind him as he ran." Perhaps Lincoln was simply young at heart.

Children and childhood played an immense role in framing Lincoln's emotional life—perhaps because he missed out on the joys of fatherly affection. His father had little use for recreational games, sports, or even academics. Abe Lincoln, on the other hand, gave himself wholeheartedly to the needs of his children—seemingly indulging himself even as he indulged them. He hugged and held them, wrestled with and tickled them, studied alongside them, and spent long hours engaging them in serious conversation. One observer wrote, "Lincoln would take his children and would walk out on the railway out in the country—would talk to them—explaining things carefully."

He enjoyed the company of his sons, and they constantly accompanied him. Most notably, after the Lincolns occupied the White House, the two youngest boys, Willie (10) and Tad (8), roamed freely. The oldest, Robert (16), had just left for Harvard. For better or worse, it was recorded that "no room was sacred from their intrusion; no conference too weighty to be broken in upon by the rush of their onslaught." They were charming, loveable, and sometimes annoying. But the president never offered a stern word or barred them from his presence. "It is my pleasure," he said, "that my children are free—happy, and unrestrained by paternal tyranny."

Senator Lyman Trumbull noted that while he was visiting Lincoln one day, their meeting was abruptly interrupted by Tad, who "when he was about six feet away . . . jumped and caught his father around the neck. Lincoln wrapped his arms about the boy . . . both of them laughing and carrying on as if there was nobody looking at them."

The rambunctious boys certainly took center stage in the daily life at the Executive Mansion. Sadly, when a typhoid epidemic swept the nation's capital, both became gravely ill. Willie did not survive, and for the first time ever or ever since, the White House ceased for a day to conduct affairs of state in order to mourn the death of a child. When Tad regained his health, the normally gruff secretary of war commissioned him as the army's youngest lieutenant—full regalia and all. The new lieutenant proceeded to drill the household staff and then ordered them to relieve the regular sentries of their watch. His amused father did not interfere, and when the young lieutenant fell asleep exhausted from the day's duties, the commander in chief carried him to bed and then promptly returned to dismiss the ill-at-ease troops from their posts.

The Lincoln boys were not the only children seen and heard at the White House. Young visitors were often given an audience with the president. Lincoln listened to them with the same attentiveness and gave as much thought to their concerns as he did to any adult who visited the White House on official business. From the young at heart he gleaned the hope and joy he needed to continue his duties, and in return they reaped immeasurable kindness. Such was the president's legacy regarding the future generation of a country going through its own severe growing pains.

Perhaps Lincoln thought of Romans 2:4—"the goodness of God leads you to repentance"—when he put forth his belief that "Love is the chain whereby to lock a child to its parent." Imagine seeing the president as his law partner William Herndon described: "Lincoln would come down to our office . . . with one or two of his little children, hauling them in the same little wagon, and in our office, then and there, write declarations, pleas, and other legal papers." Imagine your heavenly Father hauling you behind him in a wagon so you can be with him as he conducts his daily affairs.

Lincoln made time for children. He learned from them, was strengthened and encouraged by them, and saw God's love reflected in them. He learned how to tap into their joy and wonder and hope during difficult times. Perhaps he understood that our best hope resides in our children.

> Jesus said, "Let the little children come to Me, and do not forbid them; for of such is the kingdom of heaven."
>
> Matthew 19:14

10

Rise above Your Sorrows

May God give you that consolation which is beyond all earthly power.

Abraham Lincoln

When confronted with the loss of a loved one, we are shaken to the core of our innermost being. No tougher season exists than when we face great grief. Its paralyzing effects can last a lifetime.

Lincoln was no stranger to grief. It accompanied him from early childhood, through his young adult life, and into his presidency. He never escaped its grip for long. Some say that his personal losses prepared him to become the ideal leader during a period in history when great sorrow plagued the nation. He lost nearly everyone he loved most, but never did he lose his faith or allow his love of God to dim. Likewise, God can use the depth of our grief to equip us to console those who mourn, find joy in those who live, and bring strength to those around us.

An army officer who became acquainted with Lincoln once remarked, "You cannot look upon his worn, bilious, anxious countenance, and believe it to be that of a happy man." Although many think of Lincoln as a grim and stoic personality, he was equally open with his feelings of joy as well as his grief and sorrow. Seemingly in an effort to balance his uncommon sadness, he forced himself to delight in common things.

And what a great effort that must have been, especially after losing his second child. "It is hard, hard to have him die," the grieving Lincoln choked out between sobs. Lincoln stood beside the lifeless body of his eleven-year-old son, burying his head in his hands. His wife's dressmaker observed that "his tall frame convulsed with emotion." She was tending to the boy's body and later described the scene: "I stood at the foot of the bed, my eyes full of tears, looking at the man in silent, awe-stricken wonder. His grief unnerved him, and made him a weak, passive child."

When he was only nine years old, Lincoln watched close family members pass away. In the remote wilderness of Indiana where they lived, a mysterious illness swept across their camp. His aunt and uncle died in quick succession, followed by his mother. Months later, when a preacher passed through the area, the tender young Lincoln insisted that he hold a service and preach a sermon over his mother's grave.

When Lincoln was in his twenties, he fell in love with Ann Rutledge, only to lose her to typhoid fever. She was just twenty-two. Years later, a promising law student and close friend of Lincoln's, Elmer Ellsworth, became the first casualty of the Civil War. Lincoln had just received the news moments before Senator Henry Wilson and a *New York Herald* reporter entered his office. "Excuse me," he said, "but I cannot talk." Before they could inquire further, Lincoln broke into tears. He placed a handkerchief over his face and circled the room in silence. Finally he sat down, inviting the men to join him, saying, "I will make no apology, gentlemen, for my weakness. I knew poor Ellsworth well and held him in great regard." The reporter published his observation that at this the president made a "violent attempt to restrain his emotion."

Throughout all these sorrows, Lincoln continued to conduct meetings, make weighty decisions, deliver speeches, and encourage those around him. From Lincoln's letters of condolence, of which he wrote many, we learn something of the nature of his inner fortitude. When long-time friend and colleague William McCullough died while leading a raid near Coffeeville, Mississippi, Lincoln consoled the man's grieving daughter, Fanny McCullough, with the following words:

> Perfect relief is not possible, except with time. You cannot now realize that you will ever feel better. Is not this so? And yet it is a mistake. You are sure to be happy again. To know this, which is certainly true, will make you somewhat less miserable now. I have had experience enough to know what I say, and you need only believe it to feel better at once. The memory

of your dear father, instead of agony, will yet be a sad, sweet feeling in your heart, of a purer and holier sort than you have known before.

Lincoln did not let the demands of his public duties keep him from composing these private letters of encouragement. For example, he wrote to one grieving mother: "I pray that our heavenly Father may assuage the anguish of your bereavement, and leave you only the cherished memory of the loved and lost, and the solemn pride that must be yours to have laid so costly a sacrifice upon the altar of freedom."

Having felt the anguish of losing those he loved most, he was well acquainted with the sorrows of those who grieve. As was Christ, Lincoln was a man of many sorrows. Because of Christ, he knew that such sorrows were not his alone to bear—and that heaven's peace could reach deeper than any earthly grief. He made no apologies for his weaknesses or for his need to lean on Christ—nor was he ashamed to encourage others in their weakness to do the same.

> A Man of sorrows and acquainted with grief. . . .
> Surely He has borne our griefs
> And carried our sorrows. . . .
> The chastisement for our peace was upon Him.
>
> Isaiah 53:3–5

11

Be Full of Mercy

I have always found that mercy bears richer fruits than strict justice.

Abraham Lincoln

Do you practice mercy, or are you quick to judge and penalize? When we criticize other people and refuse to be lenient when they fail, we risk subjecting ourselves to the same treatment—by others and by God. God's mercy is our only hope because we all sin and fall short of his glory (Rom. 3:23). Lincoln practiced mercy to the utmost. He sought it out; he worked at it.

During a period of perpetual violence, military violations, and crimes against the state, President Lincoln issued more pardons and clemency warrants than any other president before or since. When lives hung in the balance—including every sentence of death that awaited executive order—Lincoln searched for any glimmer of evidence that justified leniency. Even when it was unpopular, he remained the single voice of mercy against the many shouts demanding the strictest justice.

He was notoriously lenient when it came to military offenses—from minor transgressions of disobedience to major acts of rebellion. Whether a soldier fell asleep on duty, abandoned his post, or even deserted his troop, Lincoln found a reason to exonerate him. Biographer Bell Irvin Wiley records: "Of all the sentences of death imposed on Union soldiers for sleeping on post that crossed Lincoln's desk for his signature, none received his approval." Regarding deserters Lincoln said, "If Almighty God gives a man a cowardly pair of legs, how can he help their running away with him?"

Lincoln only approved a very few death sentences, which he personally examined at great length. On one such occasion, Secretary John Hay noted, "Today we spent six hours deciding on Court Martials . . . I was amused at the eagerness with which the President caught at any fact which would justify him in saving the life of a condemned soldier." The president certainly didn't find anything amusing about sentencing fellow Americans to death. Author Hank Cox comments, "He never failed to see the people in the papers—whether farm boys condemned for cowardice or Indians in the shadow of the gallows—and to extend compassion wherever he could find a pretext for its purchase."

When hundreds of Sioux Indians were sentenced to hang, Lincoln gave the order to suspend execution until he personally reviewed each case. Of the 303 condemned to die, he personally wrote out the names of only 39 he found worthy of the death penalty—and still pardoned one of them. It was a risky move when his political career seemed to hang in the balance, but as he famously stated, "I could not afford to hang men for votes."

Upon receiving notice that a court tribunal had sentenced a young man to be shot the following day, Senator William Kellogg appealed to the secretary of war. After his request for clemency was denied, he went straight to the White House. Although the hour was late and the president had already retired, Kellogg pressed his way inside to Lincoln's bedside. "This man must not be shot, Mr. President! Why, he is an old neighbor of mine; I can't allow him to be shot!" Without rising from the bed, the president replied, "Well, I don't believe shooting him will do him any good."

On another occasion, during a White House reception, General Clinton Fisk met an elderly man who had been waiting in the anteroom for several days hoping to meet with the president. He had come to advocate for his son who had been sentenced to death for a military offense. General Fisk wrote an outline of the circumstances on a card and sent it to the president. Moments later, an order came that the old man be allowed to pass by the waiting senators, governors, and generals into the president's office. Upon hearing his case, Lincoln promised to consider it and to send him an answer the following day.

In desperation, the agonized father looked into the president's eyes and cried, "Tomorrow may be too late! My son is under sentence of death! The decision ought to be made now!" Lincoln, moved by his tears, gently reassured him. "Come," he said, "wait a bit, and I'll tell you a story." As the story unfolded, the old man forgot his troubles, and at its conclusion, the two men laughed aloud together. Then the president wrote out an official pardon to take with him, and the tears returned.

Lincoln valued human life more than any principle or possible promotion. As a lawyer, he firmly understood that at times the letter of the law can kill, but it is the spirit of the law that gives life (2 Cor. 3:6). As a great leader, he was strong-willed and determined but also gentle and merciful. He acted with benevolence toward people and purposed to live "with malice toward none."

> The merciful man does good for his own soul,
> But he who is cruel troubles his own flesh.
>
> Proverbs 11:17

12

Honor Your Vows

Whatever shall appear to be God's will, I will do.

Abraham Lincoln

Early in July of 1862 Lincoln approached his cabinet regarding his proposal to issue a formal proclamation emancipating the slaves. His suggestion was met with varying degrees of resistance. Some agreed that the declaration should be made, some assented to the principle but not the timing, and still others opposed it altogether. Upon the advice of Secretary of State William Seward, Lincoln agreed to temporarily table the proclamation. Secretary Seward believed that a formal move toward emancipation would be "viewed as the last measure of an exhausted government, a cry for help [for a bloody slave insurrection] . . . our last shriek on the retreat."

Throughout the months that followed, Lincoln prayed. Secretary of the Treasury Salmon Chase commented to Senator Joseph Gillespie, "It might be thought strange that he had in this way submitted the disposal of the matter when the way was not clear to his mind what he should do," but, he continued, "circumstances had happened during the war to induce him to a belief in 'special providences.'" Lincoln pleaded to God, asking what he should do. In order to be fully convinced, Lincoln vowed that if the Union army was victorious in the upcoming military campaign, he would issue the proclamation.

On September 17, near Antietam Creek outside of Sharpsburg, Maryland, the first major battle was fought on Northern soil. It was the bloodiest day of combat in American history, with nearly 23,000 casualties. Although the Union army, under Major General McClellan, outnumbered Robert E. Lee's Confederate army two-to-one, McClellan barely managed to push Lee's forces south. The Confederates withdrew to Virginia, where they successfully regrouped.

The battle at Antietam prevented the South from invading Maryland. Although small, the victory convinced Lincoln that God had revealed his will regarding emancipation. The president called a special session of the cabinet and astounded them with the following announcement: "I think the time has come now . . . the rebels have been driven out of Maryland." According to Chase, Lincoln adamantly asserted that "the time for the annunciation of the emancipation policy could no longer be delayed." Lincoln explained:

> When the rebel army was at Frederick, I determined as soon
> as it should be driven out of Maryland, to issue a Proclamation
> of Emancipation, such as I thought mostly likely to be useful. I
> said nothing to anyone, but I made the promise to myself and
> [hesitating a little] to my Maker. The rebel army is now driven
> out, and I am going to fulfill that promise.

Navy Secretary Welles also recorded in his diary that
Lincoln made it very clear "that if God gave them the victory
in the approaching battle he would consider it an indication
of the divine will and that it was his duty to move forward
in the cause of emancipation." Lincoln sought God's direction; believing he had received it, he stopped at nothing to
carry it out.

As predicted, when Lincoln's intentions to emancipate every
slave became known, there was a tremendous uprising. Twenty
percent of the slaves held by Confederate interests defected
to the North. This caused a great deal of social pressure and
subsequent unrest throughout the Northern states. Asked by
his wife what he intended to do, Lincoln looked toward the
heavens and replied, "I have my orders, I cannot do otherwise." Against tremendous opposition, he wrote, delivered, and
signed the proclamation on New Year's Day, 1863. He said, "I
never in my life felt more certain that I was doing right than
in signing this paper."

In his time of uncertainty, Lincoln sought God's counsel.
When he understood that "God had decided this question in
favor of the slaves," he did everything in his power to emancipate them. Lincoln fully believed that if he sought direction

from God, then God would answer him—and he fully intended to honor his promise to follow the direction he was given.

Our lives are no more certain, and our God is no less willing to answer when we seek him. Like Lincoln, we can recognize God's voice if we choose to listen. In those moments, it is easy to say yes to his will, but it can be a challenge to honor our commitment when we face the opinions of others, difficult circumstances, or worse, our own complacency. But like Lincoln, we can rise above these challenges and offer ourselves as vessels "useful for the Master, prepared for every good work" (2 Tim. 2:21).

> If My people who are called by My name will humble themselves, and pray and seek My face, and turn from their wicked ways, then I will hear from heaven, and will forgive their sin and heal their land.
>
> 2 Chronicles 7:14

13

BE RESOLUTE

*Always bear in mind that your resolution to succeed
is more important than any one thing.*

Abraham Lincoln

*I*f ever there were a modern-day story of David and
Goliath, it would be the Senate race of 1854. Abraham
Lincoln—then a little-known, small-town lawyer—challenged
the nationally known, well-funded, political powerhouse, Stephen Douglas. Just two years earlier, the Democratic Party
had nominated Douglas for president. The leading politician
in the dominant political party, he was now one of the most
powerful and famous men in the country. His supporters were

confident that he would be the nominee in the next presidential election.

But Lincoln was convinced that Douglas was not all that he appeared to be. "The truth is Douglas is a liar," Lincoln told Illinois congressman Thomas J. Henderson. To his law partner Clifton Moore, he said, "Douglas will tell a lie to ten thousand people one day, even though he knows he may have to deny it to five thousand the next." In addition, the candidates were divided by a deep moral disagreement regarding the issues. More than exposing Douglas or even winning the election, Lincoln sought the triumph of a moral ideal: the end of slavery. "Think nothing of me," Lincoln urged voters, "but come back to the truths that are in the Declaration of Independence. You may do anything with me you choose, if you will but heed these sacred principles."

On October 3, 1854, at the Illinois State Fair, Lincoln made his intentions known. After Douglas finished speaking in the overcrowded State Capitol building, Lincoln announced from the floor that the next day he would respond to Douglas's remarks. The following morning, handbills were distributed promoting Lincoln's rebuttal, which would take place later that afternoon. Douglas sat in the front row of the crowded Hall of Representatives as Lincoln stepped up to the podium to deliver the first of many great speeches he would make over the course of his campaign.

Throughout the following weeks, Lincoln chased Douglas around the state of Illinois. He spoke from nearby balconies—or from platforms he constructed himself—wherever Douglas had gathered a crowd. Lincoln proved to be an annoying and persistent fly in the ointment of Douglas's campaign. After being repeatedly challenged to a formal debate, Douglas agreed to a series of debates to be held in seven locations of his choosing.

Thus, the stage was set for the most famous Senate campaign in American history. Having aroused the curiosity of the public, Lincoln was propelled into the limelight. More importantly, Lincoln demonstrated his formidable debating ability, putting Douglas on the defensive. His cross-examining skills as a trial lawyer served him well, and on one occasion Douglas telegraphed an associate, "The hell-hounds are on my track. For God's sake . . . come and help me fight them."

Although the Lincoln-Douglas debates did not get Lincoln elected, they did garner a great deal of attention. "No man of this generation has grown more rapidly before the country than Lincoln in this canvas," the *New York Evening Post* announced. After losing the election, Lincoln did not allow himself to become discouraged, but professed, "The fight must go on. The cause of civil liberty must not be surrendered at the end of one, or even, one hundred defeats."

Lincoln did not allow an imposing foe, difficult circumstances, or even defeat to keep him from achieving his goal. Nor did he lose sight of his true goal. He dedicated himself to abolishing slavery regardless of whether he did it from the Senate chambers or city streets. Lincoln's strength of purpose was rooted in something greater than himself, and it was this passionate resolve that ultimately propelled him to the presidency.

As our values are challenged, how resolute are we in taking a stand for our beliefs? Whenever you encounter disappointments or setbacks, remember Lincoln's words. Just as Lincoln faced Douglas against formidable odds, you can face the daunting challenges that threaten to defeat you. If you "let no feeling of discouragement prey upon you, in the end you are sure to succeed."

> One thing I do, forgetting those things which are behind
> and reaching forward to those things which are ahead,
> I press toward the goal for the prize of the upward call
> of God in Christ Jesus.
>
> Philippians 3:13–14

14

Have Faith to the End

Let us have faith that right makes might; and in that faith let us, to the end, dare to do our duty as we understand it.

Abraham Lincoln

There are two ways to approach life; one is to live by sight, base everything on what you can see—the empirical approach. That is how most people live. The other way is to live by faith, which is to base everything on what you can't see. Lincoln lived by faith. He once wrote of the renowned British abolitionists Granville Sharp and William Wilberforce: "Though they blazed like tallow-candles for a century, at last they flickered in the socket and died out . . . and were remembered no more, even by smell. I cannot but regard it as possible that the higher object of this contest may not be completely attained within the term of my natural life. After all, whoever heard of a reformer reaping the reward of his labors in his lifetime?" Like Sharp and Wilberforce, who never saw all the fruits of their faith, Lincoln had faith to the end. Do you have such faith?

Lincoln's faith was based on what he saw as truth—as the Bible so declared. In accepting the Republican nomination for Senate in 1858, Lincoln drafted a speech that his colleagues felt would certainly end his political career. In it he begged the nation to end slavery. Against opposition, he gave the speech, telling his colleagues that he wanted to "strike home to the minds of men in order to raise them up to the peril of the times," and that if "it is decreed that I should go down because of this speech, then let me go down linked to the truth." Now that's faith!

Lincoln held an uncommon fear of God and trusted that God's purposes would ultimately prevail. He relied on God to lead him; he trusted God and placed his life in God's hands. Compared to the fate of a nation, and the role of that nation in God's sovereign plan, what value did his life have?

> I know there is a God, and that He hates injustice and slavery.
> I see the storm coming, and I know that His hand is in it. If He
> has a place and work for me—and I think He has—I believe I
> am ready. I am nothing, but truth is everything. I know I am
> right because I know that liberty is right, for Christ teaches
> it, and Christ is God.

As long as God gave him breath, Lincoln committed himself to speaking out on behalf of freedom. He trusted that God had ordained him to further his deeply held beliefs and that God would help him. And God did. Lincoln overcame insurmountable odds, he swayed his opposition, he rallied a great force of supporters to join him—sometimes in spite of themselves, and he awoke a sleeping nation. He had faith that the Union would be preserved despite a war that had claimed the lives of 618,000 soldiers—more lives than were lost in every other American war from the Revolution to the invasion of Iraq. Lincoln had faith that a backwoods boy could become president, even after losing several campaigns in a row. Most significantly, Lincoln had faith that the institution of slavery in America would end, even if he did not live to see it:

> Douglas doesn't care whether slavery is voted up or voted down, but God cares, and humanity cares, and I care; and with God's help I shall not fail. I may not see the end; but it will come, and I shall be vindicated; and these men will find that they have not read their Bibles aright.

Lincoln had faith that God's truth would ultimately prevail.

After Lincoln became president, his faith was tested even further. He lost his second youngest son to a prolonged fever while the youngest still lay in bed battling for his life. Speaking to his children's nurse, Mrs. Rebecca Pomeroy, who had offered some words of prayer and comfort to the grieving Lincoln, he replied, "I wish I had the childlike faith you speak of, and I trust He will give it to me." And God again proved himself

70

faithful by completing the good work—and the faith—he had begun in Lincoln.

God is still at work today, moving in his people's hearts by his Spirit of truth (see John 16:13). The just are still called to live by faith (Rom. 1:17; Gal. 3:11; Heb. 10:38), and Jesus is still the author and finisher of that faith (Heb. 12:2). Now more than ever, we must exercise the measure of faith given to us to change the course of our nation. Let Lincoln's exhortation inspire you to act in opposition to the peril of the times: "All you have to do is keep the faith, to remain steadfast in the right, to stand by your banner. Nothing should lead you to leave your guns. Stand together, match in hand. Allow nothing to turn you to the right or the left."

> Therefore we also, since we are surrounded by so great a cloud of witnesses . . . let us run with endurance the race that is set before us, looking unto Jesus, the author and finisher of our faith.
>
> Hebrews 12:1–2

15

Champion Equality

Who shall say, "I am the superior, and you are the inferior"?

Abraham Lincoln

The Bible teaches that there is no respecter of persons with God. The Scriptures are replete with teaching that God does not favor one person over another. He created all men equal. How do you see it? Are you a respecter of persons?

In May of 1831 twenty-two-year-old Lincoln found himself in the bustling port city of New Orleans. Here he came face-to-face with the cruelty of the slave trade when he observed men and women being paraded about and auctioned off like animals in open markets. The human degradation left an indelible mark on Lincoln's soul.

Long-time friend and law partner William Herndon wrote that "in New Orleans for the first time, Lincoln beheld the true horrors of human slavery. He saw Negroes in chains—whipped and scourged." After residing in the city for a month, Lincoln came to a strikingly clear understanding of the ethics—or lack thereof—surrounding the issue of slavery. "Against this inhumanity his sense of right and justice rebelled, and his mind and conscience were awakened to a realization of what he had often heard and read. Slavery ran the iron into him then and there."

On one memorable occasion, Lincoln passed by the slave markets while a mulatto girl was being auctioned for sale. She was publicly examined from head to toe and forced to trot up and down the platform like a horse "to show how she moved." Herndon records that "the whole thing was so revolting that Lincoln moved away from the scene with a deep feeling of 'unconquerable hate.' He said, 'Boys, let's get away from this. If ever I get a chance to hit that thing' (meaning slavery) 'I'll hit it hard.'"

Lincoln saw slavery as an evil that had wound its way down through the centuries in various forms. In an 1858 campaign speech he said, "The same old serpent that says you work and I eat, you toil and I will enjoy the fruits of it. . . . Turn it whatever way you will—whether it come from the mouth of a King [as] an excuse for enslaving the people of his country, or from the mouth of men of one race as a reason for enslaving the men of another race, it is the same old serpent."

Lincoln compared slave owners to the evil despots that Americans condemned in the Declaration of Independence. His comment that kings were enslavers of their subjects was intended to arouse memories of why colonial America broke away from British oppressors in the first place. The free citizens of the United States were inflicting the same type of cruelty upon an entire race of people that had led to a revolution less than a century earlier. In June of 1857 in Springfield, Illinois, Lincoln made these comments regarding the Declaration of Independence:

> I think the authors of that notable instrument intended to include all men, but they did not intend to declare all men equal in all respects. They did not mean to say all men were equal in color, size, intellect, moral development or social capacity. They defined with tolerable distinction in what respects they did consider all men created equal—equal with "certain inalienable rights, among which are life, liberty and the pursuit of happiness."

To Lincoln, this represented a universal ideal that was worth defending, even to the point of death. He remembered when he was a boy hearing the story of the Revolutionary army crossing the ice-choked Delaware River in a driving sleet storm on Christmas night 1776, in order to attack the British garrison at Trenton. "I recollect thinking then . . . that there must have been something more than common that those men struggled for . . . something even more than National Independence . . . something that held out a great promise to all the people of the world for all time to come . . . that in due time the weights should be lifted from the shoulders of all men, and that all should have an equal chance."

In 1863 African-American abolitionist Frederick Douglass and Lincoln met for the first time. Douglass recalled that Lincoln was "the first great man that I talked with in the United States who in no single instance reminded me of the difference between himself and myself, of the difference of color."

Although the color of one's skin might not seem like a cause for debate today, other factors compel us to make judgments about equality. Not everyone is equal—that is, identical—in all respects, but all of us would benefit by remembering that *all* people *are* created with "certain inalienable rights, among which are life, liberty and the pursuit of happiness."

> And Peter opened his mouth and said: Most certainly and thoroughly I now perceive and understand that God shows no partiality and is no respecter of persons.
>
> Acts 10:34 AMP

16

PREPARE FOR YOUR DESTINY

I will prepare and some day my chance will come.

Abraham Lincoln

*E*ven as a child, Abe Lincoln was a bit of an enigma. He didn't quite fit into his surroundings. From the Indiana backwoods, to the small town of New Salem, Illinois, to the courtrooms of Springfield, to the White House—he always seemed at odds with his environment, moving against the current in some deliberate way. He was often misunderstood, often a cause of wonder—sometimes even amusement—but most often a source of inspiration as he marched to the beat of his own drum with a cadenced determination. He acted as if he were created for a special purpose.

"Abe was awful lazy . . . he was always reading and thinking—used to get mad at him," Lincoln's former neighbor and employer, John Romine, once told William Herndon. Lincoln's cousin Dennis Hanks reported that "Lincoln was lazy—a very lazy man—he was always reading—scribbling—writing—ciphering—writing poetry, etc." His stepmother, Sarah Bush Lincoln, summed it up this way: "He didn't like physical labor. [He] was diligent for knowledge—wished to know and if pain and labor would get it he was sure to get it." Lincoln's stepsister, Matilda, said, "Abe was not energetic except in one thing—he was active and persistent in learning—read everything he could."

Young Abe Lincoln must have been frustrated by the lack of formal education available to him. A good school was one of many important necessities missing from Lincoln's childhood. But he did not let his environment or lack of support hinder his intellectual growth. As a natural-born scholar, he soon out-learned his school headmasters in the remote areas of Indiana. As a lanky preadolescent, Lincoln walked as far as eight miles in search of a book he hadn't already read.

Biographer William Barton records that according to his longtime friend and colleague Leonard Swett, "He borrowed and read every book he could learn about within a circuit of fifty miles. Among those borrowed volumes was a copy of the *Revised Statutes of Indiana*, the beginning of his reading the law." But all the knowledge in the world would profit him little if he couldn't speak and write correctly, so before his twentieth birthday, he walked six miles to obtain a copy of Samuel Kirkham's *English Grammar*.

His love for learning impressed his stepmother, who confirmed that "Abe read all the books he could lay his hand on—and when he came across a passage that struck him he would write it down on boards if he had no paper and [would] keep it there till he did get paper—then he would rewrite it—look at it—repeat it—he had a copy book—a kind of scrap book in which he put down all things and this preserved them." A New Salem friend, Robert Rutledge, wrote, "His practice was, when he wished to indelibly fix any thing he was reading or studying on his mind, to write it down. [I've] known him to write whole pages of books he was reading."

After passing the bar and establishing his law practice, Lincoln taught himself Euclid's geometric principles. He did this while "tramping around the Eighth Circuit as a lawyer because he wanted to discipline his mind." He proudly claimed that he "mastered the Six-books of Euclid." His first law partner, John Stuart, recalled that "he read hard works—was philosophical, logical, mathematical—never read generally." Fellow circuit rider Leonard Swett observed: "Life was to him a school and he was always studying and mastering every subject which came before him."

As president and commander in chief of the army and navy, he borrowed books on military strategy from the Library of Congress. "Some of the most dramatic events in Lincoln's presidency grew out of his direct intervention in strategic and command decisions." Lincoln never lost his thirst for knowledge or his love for learning. He believed his duty was to prepare for his destiny. Even at the height of achievement, as United States president, he continued to read, learn, and grow. "You can not fail in any laudable object unless you allow your mind to be improperly directed," Lincoln wrote to William Herndon. "The way for a man to rise is to improve himself every way he can." For Lincoln, destiny prepared was destiny served. It's an important lesson we often forget. We want to believe there is a special purpose for our lives, but we fail to prepare for it. Possibly the degree to which we find our destiny is the degree to which we get ready for it.

> Study and be eager and do your utmost to present your-
> self to God approved, a workman who has no cause to
> be ashamed, correctly analyzing and accurately dividing
> the Word of Truth.
>
> 2 Timothy 2:15 AMP

17

LOVE YOUR SPOUSE

Love is eternal.

Abraham Lincoln

An old adage tells us that opposites attract. Do you ever feel as if you're hopelessly the opposite of your spouse in certain ways? Over time, our novel and charming differences can grow into colossal annoyances. Every marriage faces this challenge. Too often, couples fail to rise to these challenges and instead divorce, but not Abe and Mary. They serve as an example to all married couples. They stuck through the challenges together.

Like most married couples, Abe and Mary were quite different from each other. Mary Todd Lincoln was as flamboyant as

Abe was simple. While Abe was known for his quiet reserve and introspection, she had a reputation for being "high strung, nervous, impulsive, excitable." People knew Lincoln as steady, composed, and unflappable; Mary, however, was "sunning all over with laughter one moment, the next crying as though her heart would break," according to her cousin Margaret Stuart. Longtime friend O. H. Browning commented, "She was always either in the garret or cellar."

No doubt Mary's extreme and frequent mood swings placed additional stress on their marriage. Lincoln was known to endure her outbursts by emotionally withdrawing, taking the children on long walks, or escaping to his office, where he could sleep on his couch. His strategy was to ignore her, and sometimes when she experienced "one of her nervous spells," he stayed away from home for days at a time. Some historians have speculated that if his domestic situation had been happier, he might not have been so interested in campaigning for public office with all the travel it required.

On one occasion, Mary slapped a young maid across the face for displeasing her. To make things worse, when the young lady's father inquired about the incident, Mary went after him, wildly swinging a broom handle. When the furious man at last tracked down Lincoln to complain, Lincoln slowly shook his head and replied, "Can't you endure this one wrong done you while I have had to bear it without complaint for lo these many years?" The suddenly sympathetic man immediately dropped the matter.

But beneath her fiery temper and occasional hysterics, she truly believed in her husband. Some have suggested that Lincoln was sustained by his wife's unflagging belief that a glorious destiny awaited him. Lincoln's law partner noted that "she had the fire, will, and ambition" that perhaps Lincoln lacked. William Herndon likened Lincoln's ambition to a "little engine that knew no rest," which was continually retooled at home, because his wife was "in fact endowed with a more restless ambition than he." In his 1939 biography, *The Growth of Lincoln's Faith*, H. H. Horner wrote, "The full part her ambition for him played in keeping his own zeal alive and in holding him to a steady course, in spite of defeats and disappointments, can never be known."

Interestingly, years earlier when Mary and Abe were still courting, Mary commented on a friend of hers who had married a wealthy businessman. She said, "I would rather marry a good man—a man of mind—with a hope and bright prospects ahead for position, fame, and power—than to marry all the houses, gold, and bones in the world." Of her former suitor, Stephen Douglas, she remarked that he was a "very little, little giant, by the side of my tall Kentuckian, and intellectually my husband towers above Douglas just as he does physically." In Mary's mind, her husband had "no equal in the United States."

In many ways Mary and Abe were suited for each other. Both loved learning, politics, and poetry. Both were well-read and ambitious, and both loved their boys with equal abandon. They also had weaknesses and shortcomings that were strengthened and compensated for by the other person. And both required a great deal of grace. Lincoln was absent for weeks at a time—sometimes for over half the days in the year—during their eighteen years of marriage. Between the requirements of traveling the judicial circuit as a Springfield lawyer and touring the country campaigning as a presidential nominee, Lincoln was not the doting husband he could have been.

Lincoln may have been absent, withdrawn, or seemingly insensitive, yet throughout all of his domestic trials, he never wavered in his commitment to his wife. Rather than complain, he endured their struggles with a patience and steadiness not found in many marriages today. Although Lincoln and his wife differed greatly in their temperaments, they understood their need for each other.

The Bible portrays marriage as a representation of the relationship between Jesus and his bride, the church (Eph. 5:25–27). Scripture also says God's strength is perfected in our weakness (2 Cor. 12:9). Could it be that our spouse's weaknesses perfect our strengths and vice versa?

> "For this reason a man shall leave his father and mother and be joined to his wife, and the two shall become one flesh"; so then they are no longer two, but one flesh. Therefore what God has joined together, let not man separate.
>
> Mark 10:7–9

18

BE FEARLESS UNDER FIRE

*It often requires more courage to dare to do right than
to fear to do wrong.*

Abraham Lincoln

Lincoln watched the approaching Confederate troops
as he looked through his field glasses from the front
parapet of Fort Stevens, just outside of Washington, DC. "He
stood there with a long frock coat and plug hat on, making a very
conspicuous figure," recalled signal officer Asa Townsend Abbott.
When the enemy advanced to within 150 yards of the fort, bullets
began flying through the air, one narrowly missing the president.
Then a bullet struck a nearby soldier, forcing Lincoln to relin-
quish his post. He calmly descended the parapet and mounted

his carriage to ride back to the city. He proceeded directly to the wharf to greet the arriving troops of the Sixth Corps.

"There was no fear or timidity in Mr. Lincoln's makeup," reported Captain David Derickson of Company K. "In fact," he added, "I thought him rather careless or thoughtless as to his personal safety." Lincoln's lack of fear when walking the grounds at night without an escort, strolling a beach held by the Confederates near Norfolk, or walking the streets of Richmond only hours after rebel forces withdrew astounded his contemporaries. Lincoln biographer Gary Prokopowics proposed the following explanation:

> To be an effective wartime leader, Lincoln believed he had to show his own personal bravery, his own courage in some way, since he could not do so on the battlefield. He had to demonstrate a willingness to share the risks of what he as president was requiring so many thousands of others to do.

But Lincoln not only placed himself in harm's way as commander in chief overseeing the war effort, he faced every public appearance as well as private audience with the knowledge that growing numbers of assassins were plotting to kill him. Letters threatening his life poured into the White House by the thousands. Daily Lincoln was forced to read the grave intentions of adversaries who wanted him dead. Lincoln dismissed all such plots, believing that "assassination of public officers is not an American crime."

While freely roaming the grounds of the Capitol or the streets of the city, he reasoned that he could do little to prevent someone from killing him if he or she really wanted to. "I cannot discharge my duties [in order to] withdraw myself entirely from danger of an assault," he told his secretary, John Nicolay. "I see hundreds of strangers every day, and if anybody has the disposition to kill me he will find opportunity. To be absolutely safe I should lock myself up in a box." Even so, guards surrounded Lincoln, and he was told that he should not cross the lawn from the White House to the War Department without a bodyguard. Nevertheless, Lincoln amused himself by devising ways of eluding his protectors.

When Major General Christopher Augur tried to beef up the White House escort detail with an extra company of cavalry in July of 1864, Lincoln sent their captain back with "a verbal order that the men were not wanted." The following week, the Confederate army advanced on Fort Stevens just outside Washington, DC, with Lincoln insisting on watching the battle on the fort's parapet—in full view of rebel snipers. Perhaps this was one of those critical times he was referring to when he remarked, "I, who am not a specially brave man, have had to sustain the sinking courage of those professional fighters in critical times."

Throughout his presidency, under the shadow of war and the threat of assassination, Lincoln stood tall and walked boldly through the many dangerous situations he faced. His actions reflected his moral resolve. He understood that he had to model the beliefs he unflinchingly proclaimed: "The probability that we may fail in the struggle ought not to deter us from the support of a cause we believe to be just; it shall not deter me."

Do you stand up for what you believe in, or are you sometimes too timid to draw a line in the sand? Like Lincoln, we can walk boldly in God's presence through our own trials and tribulations—even against the enemy. There is no room for timidity when in battle.

> Have I not commanded you? Be strong and courageous.
> Do not be terrified; do not be discouraged, for the Lord
> your God will be with you wherever you go.
>
> Joshua 1:9 NIV

19

Value Your Friends

The better part of one's life consists of his friendships.

Abraham Lincoln

When announcing his candidacy for the state legislature in 1832, Abraham Lincoln described the source of his political aspirations. "Every man is said to have his peculiar ambition. Whether it be true or not, I can say for one that I have no other so great as that of being truly esteemed of my fellow men, by rendering myself worthy of their esteem."

Lincoln went on to admit that "I am young and unknown to many of you. I was born and have ever remained in the most humble walks of life. I have no wealthy or popular relations to recommend me." He signed off with, "Your friend and fellow-citizen."

Lincoln, as always, spoke the truth. And although he may have had little else, he had friends, friends who propelled him to the presidency. "Wherever he moved he found men and women to respect and love him. One man who knew him at that time says that 'Lincoln had nothing, only plenty of friends.' And these friends trusted him wholly, and were willing to be led by him," wrote Josiah G. Holland, one of Lincoln's early biographers. "People were glad to see him rise, because it seemed just that he should rise. Indeed, all seemed glad to help him along."

Another early biographer and one of Lincoln's many close friends, Isaac Arnold, wrote that Lincoln "loved and trusted and confided in the people to a degree rarely known in a statesman. He had faith in the common everyday folk, with a yearning for their happiness almost paternal. The people seemed to feel instinctively how thoroughly he trusted them, and they revered and trusted him in turn." A reporter for the *New York Herald*, a newspaper known for its bias against Abraham Lincoln, filed the following description of him in February 1861:

> Putting prejudice aside, no one can see Mr. Lincoln without recognizing in him a man of immense power and force of character and natural talent. He seems so sincere, so conscientious, so simple hearted, that no one can help liking him and esteeming any disparagement of his ability or desire to do right, as a personal insult.

Indeed, his affability endeared him to many from the time when he left home in 1831 at the age of twenty-two. William Lee Miller, author of *Lincoln's Virtues*, writes that although Lincoln was endowed with an unusual confidence and intellectual ability, "it is striking how rapidly his life opens out and heads upward. How easily doors open for him. How few barriers there appear to be. How readily he finds sponsors and supporters—including persons in the upper ranks of New Salem and Springfield." Biographer Ida Tarbell concurs: "Lincoln's simple, sincere friendliness and his quaint humor soon won him a sure, social position in Washington."

Lincoln once said, "If you would win a man to your cause, first convince him that you are his sincere friend." And that appears to be what Lincoln did. His friends rallied to secure his nomination for president. Lincoln also proved loyal in his support of them. He once wrote to the accusatory political activist William Butler, "I am willing to pledge myself in black and white to cut my own throat from ear to ear, if, when I meet you, you shall seriously say, that you believe me capable of betraying my friends for any price." He signed the letter, "Your Friend, in spite of your ill-nature."

Indeed, he even befriended the friendless. When nobody else was willing to say a kind word to or about the widely criticized General Henry Halleck, Lincoln purposefully showed himself to be his "friend because nobody else was." He explained to a congressional colleague that "the man who has no friends should be taken care of." Lincoln was, according to J. Rowan Herndon, a New Salem acquaintance, "A friend to all and all a friend to him." Herndon added that Mr. Lincoln was the "favorite of all . . . men and women and children. . . . He loved all of them as they loved him."

During times of great conflict, loss, and opposition, Lincoln was friendly, faithful, and forgiving—even under the most dire circumstances or with the most distressing individuals. In a society with even greater diversity and equal cause for offense, we can follow in Lincoln's footsteps by being a friend to all, by taking time to value and enjoy our friendships, by being a friend to the friendless, and by showing kindness to those who oppose us.

> Greater love has no one than this, that he lay down his life for his friends.
>
> John 15:13 NIV

20

Be Honest No Matter the Cost

Resolve to be honest in all events; and if in your judg-
ment you cannot be an honest lawyer, resolve to be
honest without being a lawyer.

Abraham Lincoln

At the end of a long day operating the general store in New Salem, young Abe waited on his last customer. He had been on his feet since early morning and was looking forward to closing up for the night. After the woman left the store with her purchases, he carefully totaled her bill one last time to check his calculation. To his dismay, he discovered he had overcharged her six and a quarter cents. He quickly closed the store, locked the door, and walked directly to the customer's house nearly three miles away to return the difference.

Such stories of Abe's deep-seated integrity abound. A similar incident occurred near closing time at the same store. Abe weighed half a pound of tea for a customer before locking up for the evening. The next morning, he found a four-ounce weight sitting on the same scale where he had weighed the tea. He quickly measured the difference on the scale, shut down the store, and personally delivered the remainder of the tea.

In his 1908 biography, *The Story-Life of Lincoln*, author Wayne Whipple wrote about young Abe's year at Denton Offutt's store: "It was while he was performing the work at the store that he acquired the sobriquet, 'honest Abe'—a characterization that he never dishonored, and an abbreviation that he never outgrew." Whipple describes how this young man began finding his unique niche in society:

> He was judge, arbitrator, referee, umpire, authority, in all disputes, games and matches of man-flesh, horse-flesh, a pacificator in all quarrels; everybody's friend; the best-natured, the most sensible, the best-informed, the most modest and unassuming, the kindest, gentlest, roughest, strongest, best fellow in all New Salem and the region round about.

R. B. Rutledge, son of a New Salem tavern owner, recalled that "Mr. Lincoln's judgment was final in all that region of the country. People relied implicitly upon his honesty, integrity, and impartiality."

His reputation both preceded and followed him. For a time, Lincoln served as the postmaster in New Salem, Illinois. During that period, he suffered great financial hardship as he educated himself in preparation for the bar exam. All the while, he remained faithful in his duties overseeing the post office until it was moved to Petersburg. After his service as postmaster came to a close, he moved to Springfield to set up his law practice.

Years later, a postal agent found Lincoln in his law office. The agent was collecting a balance due from the now-closed New Salem office. For a moment Lincoln looked perplexed, but then he walked across the room and pulled a small box from a pile of books. Inside the box was a package of coins wrapped in a cotton rag. Lincoln counted the exact sum—more than seventeen dollars—and gave it to the agent. After the agent left, Lincoln was heard to remark that he never used any man's money but his own. "Although this sum had been in his hands during all these years, he had never regarded it as available, even for any temporary purpose of his own." He refused to "borrow" the money, despite his financial hardship.

Another close friend, Colonel Lamon, concurred that Lincoln had zero tolerance for anything deceptive or hypocritical. As a lawyer, he could not bring himself to defend a client or a cause that was not just. If necessary, he brought in another lawyer to defend a case that was less than honorable. Lamon stated that "for a man who was for a quarter of a century both a lawyer and a politician, Mr. Lincoln was the most honest man I ever knew. He was not only morally honest but intellectually so. He could not reason falsely; if he attempted it he failed. In politics he would never try to mislead." He then recounted a case where Lincoln, upon hearing the arguments of the prosecuting attorney, suddenly disappeared from the courtroom. When found at his hotel, Lincoln answered, "Tell the judge that I can't come; my hands are dirty and I came over to clean them."

During a debate in Charleston in 1858, Lincoln declared, "If I have made any assertion not warranted by facts, and it is pointed out to me, I will withdraw it cheerfully." Lincoln's honesty was rooted in his humility. Proverbs 15:33 tells us that "before honor comes humility" (NASB). If we desire to be honorable people, we must learn to humble ourselves to the truth. If we desire to walk in that truth, we must learn to fear God. At Lincoln's funeral, the Reverend Phillips Brooks gave this insight into the deceased president:

> He showed us how to love truth and yet be charitable—how to hate wrong and all oppression, and yet not treasure one personal injury or insult. . . . He spread before us the love and fear of God just in that shape in which we need them most, and out of his faithful service of a higher Master, who of us has not taken and eaten and grown strong? "He fed them with a faithful and true heart."

> If I have walked with falsehood,
>   Or if my foot has hastened to deceit,
> Let me be weighed on honest scales,
>   That God may know my integrity.

> Job 31:5–6

21

MAKE PEACE

We are not enemies, but friends. We must not be enemies. Though passion may have strained, it must not break our bonds of affection.

Abraham Lincoln

I want peace; I want to stop this terrible waste of life and property," Lincoln told James Gilmore in 1863. As a man of peace, Lincoln felt very uneasy about the necessity of war. He longed for peace for all races under the banner of a unified country, and he willingly engaged in a war to achieve it. "No man desires peace more than I," he wrote in an unfinished letter on September 12, 1864. Lincoln confided to House Speaker Alexander R. Boteler, who later became a

Confederate colonel, "I am extremely anxious to see these sectional troubles settled peaceably and satisfactorily to all concerned. To accomplish that, I am willing to make almost any sacrifice, and do anything in reason consistent with my sense of duty."

Lincoln was predisposed to achieving a peaceful resolution to disagreements, from minor quarrels to acts of war. If at all possible, he sought peace with his adversaries. "Quarrel not at all," he advised a young Captain James M. Cutts in 1863. "No man resolved to make the most of himself can spare time for personal contention." His advice sounds like the wise counsel of King Solomon: "A hot-tempered man stirs up strife, but he who is slow to anger quiets contention" (Prov. 15:18 ESV).

Back in Springfield, Lincoln was a beloved mentor to aspiring young lawyers. In one lecture, he advised them to "discourage litigation. Persuade your neighbors to compromise whenever you can. Point out to them how the nominal winner is often a real loser—in fees, expenses, and waste of time." He went on to explain that "As a peacemaker the lawyer has a superior opportunity of being a good man. There will be business enough." Compare the reputation of the legal profession today with Lincoln's observations in 1850:

> Never stir up litigation. A worse man can scarcely be found than one who does this. Who can be more nearly a fiend than he who habitually overhauls the register of deeds in search of defects in titles, whereon to stir up strife, and put money in his pocket? A moral tone ought to be infused into the profession which should drive such men out of it.

Lincoln was respected for his services as a local mediator. He once wrote to client Abram Bale, "I sincerely hope you will settle it. I think you *can* if you *will*, for I have always found Mr. Hickox a fair man in his dealings. If you settle I will charge nothing for what I have done, and thank you to boot." Lincoln made every effort to settle court claims through mediation and compromise. Throughout the Eighth Judicial Circuit, he resolved disputes among citizens, negotiated public apologies, and often convinced the disputing parties to equally divide any court costs.

Slander cases were especially abhorrent to Lincoln at a time when defamation-of-character accusations proliferated. As president, he needed thick skin to endure the personal insults he often incurred. In a famous incident recorded by preacher-turned-statesman Rev. Owen Lovejoy, Lincoln did not hesitate to humble himself in order to maintain a friendship with another person. Lovejoy found himself caught in the middle of a disagreement between Lincoln and Secretary of War Edwin Stanton. Lincoln had sent a note via Lovejoy suggesting a transfer of regiments, to which Stanton replied:

"Did Lincoln give you an order of that kind?"

"He did, sir," responded Lovejoy.

"Then he is a damned fool," thundered Stanton.

"Do you mean to say the president is a damned fool?" asked Lovejoy.

"Yes, sir, if he gave you such an order as that."

Back in Lincoln's office, Lovejoy recounted his conversation with Stanton. "Did Stanton say I was a damned fool?" Lincoln asked. "He did, sir, and repeated it," said Lovejoy. The president pondered for a moment and then remarked, "If Stanton said I was a damned fool, then I must be one, for he is nearly always right, and generally says what he means. I will step over and see him." Lincoln did not take offense but sought to understand his accuser's point of view.

In his First Inaugural Address, on March 4, 1861, Lincoln revealed his insight into human nature and the effort required to work toward harmony. He understood the sacrifices needed but also the victory that would eventually prevail once the national conflict was resolved.

> We are not enemies, but friends. We must not be enemies. Though passion may have strained, it must not break our bonds of affection. The mystic chords of memory, stretching from every battlefield and patriot grave to every living heart and hearthstone all over this broad land, will yet swell the chorus of the Union, when again touched, as surely they will be, by the better angels of our nature.

In times of discord, we can choose to seek peace. Although we may be right (at least in our own minds), if we desire to live holy lives, we must "pursue peace with all people" (Heb. 12:14). After all, as followers of Christ we have been given the "ministry of reconciliation"—because in Christ, God reconciled the world to himself, "not imputing their trespasses to them" (2 Cor. 5:18–19). How much more then should we seek to be reconciled with those who have offended us?

We would do well to remember the lessons found throughout Psalms and Proverbs warning of fools and evildoers who stir up strife, and praising the wise and just who seek peace.

Peter reminds us of the psalmist's admonition, "Let him turn away from evil and do good; Let him seek peace and pursue it" (1 Peter 3:11). Avoid being contentious and heed the words of Jesus: "Blessed are the peacemakers, for they shall be called sons of God" (Matt. 5:9 ESV).

> But the wisdom that is from above is first pure, then peaceable, gentle, willing to yield, full of mercy and good fruits, without partiality and without hypocrisy. Now the fruit of righteousness is sown in peace by those who make peace.
>
> James 3:17–18

22

OVERCOME YOUR DESPAIR

It is difficult to make a man miserable while he feels worthy of himself and claims kindred to the great God who made him.

Abraham Lincoln

Do you sometimes feel defeated or rejected by circumstances in your life? Lincoln learned to rise above his despair. When a man named John Widmer heard that Abe Lincoln was in town to argue a case before the Supreme Court, he walked to the courtroom to watch. The "lank, gaunt figure thoughtfully studying the floor" made an unusual impression on him. Widmer observed Lincoln's "very pale, long face, big hands and feet," but what stood out most was "the extreme sadness of his eyes. Lincoln had the saddest eyes of any human being that I have ever seen." Widmer stated that "His melancholy expression had so impressed me that I should not have felt more solemn if I had been at a funeral."

A fellow lawyer, Orlando B. Ficklin, explained that the pictures we see of Lincoln "only half represent him." He makes the interesting observation that seeing Lincoln "in motion of storytelling, and then falling back into misery, made the latter state all the more dramatic." Lincoln balanced a pervasive melancholy with humorous stories. But he also experienced moments when his sadness overwhelmed him. He battled serious bouts of depression and thoughts of suicide. However mentally unstable he may have appeared at times, an inner fortitude endowed him with an almost unimaginable strength and courage.

Given the grave times in which he lived, the losses and hardships he endured, and his personal shortcomings that were directly at odds with his personal ambition, it is no wonder he felt glum. Consider the deaths that pursued him throughout his life: the loss of an infant brother when Lincoln was three years old; the death of his mother, aunt, and uncle at age nine; his sister's passing at eighteen; his first true love while still in his twenties; a four-year-old son, Edward; and then his beloved twelve-year-old Willie, who was reputed to be "just like his father." It was enough to prompt a lifetime of melancholy.

Some have supposed that Lincoln was genetically predisposed to depression. His father, uncle, and cousins were known for their moody spells and periods of extreme melancholy. One of Lincoln's first cousins, Mary Jane, was committed to the Illinois State Hospital for the Insane by a jury that concluded "the disease is with her heredity." Lincoln described his mother as "intellectual, sensitive, and somewhat sad."

During the winter of 1840–41 Lincoln appeared to fight for his sanity after suffering a series of professional and personal crises. His political reputation had been discredited by his adamant defense of an expensive "internal improvement scheme" for the state of Illinois, which ultimately destroyed the state's economy. On January 1, 1841, the debt interest that the state owed was due—a day Lincoln referred to as "the fatal first." It was also the day he broke off his engagement to Mary Todd. During the next few weeks he suffered what many believe was a complete mental collapse.

Three weeks later, he wrote his law partner John Stuart in Washington, DC:

> I am now the most miserable man living. If what I feel were equally distributed to the whole human family, there would not be one cheerful face on the earth. Whether I shall ever be better I can not tell; I awfully forebode I shall not. To remain as I am is impossible; I must die or be better, it appears to me.

In *Lincoln's Melancholy* Joshua Wolf Shenk claims that this was a significant turning point for Lincoln. It represented a type of crucible that marked "the end of Lincoln's youth with its dramatic fits of public melancholy, and the beginning of his manhood, with a quiet, weary suffering that many witnessed but few could understand." Shenk further explains that this period "marked the end of his startling rise as a provincial politician and the beginning of a long, slow trudge to find a voice in the affairs of the nation."

And that is what happened. Lincoln found his voice and completely threw himself into the national political arena. He stood for his deeply held beliefs of freedom and unity. Although the Civil War consumed him, eventually taking his life, it provided an "emotional outlet in which he could immerse his own psyche. . . . Having to worry about other people's problems took his mind off his own."

> Lincoln was surrounded by chaos during the war years. He strongly embraced one basic proposition: to preserve the Union. In his Gettysburg Address, he asserted "a new birth of freedom." For Lincoln, the concept of a democratic America symbolized "the last, best hope of earth." The basic, yet weighty concept, defined the essence of this conflict: there would be no compromise. We can't help but ask: was his approach to the war a symbiotic expression, based on his personal approach to the idiosyncratic tragedies of his own life?

Lincoln needed something bigger than himself to pull him out of the depths of his despair. It took the enormity of the Civil War—and the embrace of a heavenly Father—to keep him from sinking into those depths. The intensity of Lincoln's emotional experience suited him well for the time and place to which he was called. His innate ability to "hope against hope" when dark forces threatened to destroy his world—both within and without—steeled him, making him stronger. Shenk concludes that "Lincoln didn't do great work because he solved the problem of his melancholy. The problem of his melancholy was all the more fuel for the fire of his great work."

When his good friend Joshua Speed suffered from the ills of a "nervous temperament," Lincoln observed that while the general cause was hereditary, "three special causes" compounded the general one. From his advice to Speed, we catch a glimpse of Lincoln's studied insight into his own experience:

> The first special cause is your exposure to bad weather on your journey, which my experience clearly proves to be very severe on defective nerves.
>
> The second is, the absence of all business and conversation of friends, which might divert your mind, and give it occasional rest from that intensity of thought, which will sometimes wear the sweetest idea thread-bare and turn it to the bitterness of death.
>
> The third is, the rapid and near approach of that crisis on which all your thoughts and feelings concentrate.

We can all benefit by reflecting on Lincoln's "special causes" for anxiety. Certainly the weather plays on our emotions. And staying busy and socializing with our colleagues and friends are cures for the blues. But most importantly, as those dreaded moments approach that dominate our thoughts, we can heed the apostle Paul's advice: "by prayer and petition, with thanksgiving, present your requests to God. And the peace of God, which transcends all understanding, will guard your hearts and your minds in Christ Jesus" (Phil. 4:6–7 NIV).

Finally, brothers, whatever is true, whatever is noble, whatever is right, whatever is pure, whatever is lovely, whatever is admirable—if anything is excellent or praise-worthy—think about such things. . . . And the God of peace will be with you.

Philippians 4:8–9 NIV

23

WORK HARD

The leading rule is diligence. Leave nothing for tomorrow which can be done today.

Abraham Lincoln

Do other people say you are a hard worker? Do you press on toward the mark? Lincoln's willingness to work hard quickly distinguished him from his peers. Perhaps his strong work ethic contributed to his reputation for honesty and humility—after all, deceitfulness and pride are the hallmarks of laziness. From his youth, he was not above doing whatever was necessary to achieve a goal—from walking twenty miles to borrow a book, to learning obscure calculations, to becoming a land surveyor. Lincoln exhibited initiative and foresight along with the ability to discern where he wanted to go and what needed to be done to get there.

Industrious and innovative, Lincoln invested himself in relentless self-improvement. In order to change the course of his life from farming the land to leading the nation, he molded himself into the kind of man to whom people would trust their future. He overcame his background, his lack of education, the way he talked, and even how he looked. Lincoln trained his mind; he taught himself how to speak, how to conduct himself in society, and how to build lasting and meaningful relationships. He worked hard at making and keeping friends, at sustaining his marriage, and at building his career.

Lincoln made the most of every opportunity to build on what he knew; what he didn't know, he taught himself. He knew the Sangamon River, so he became a flatboat pilot, making his way to New Salem. Not much later he became the pilot of a steamboat navigating the vessel's maiden voyage to the banks of Springfield. A job well done often led to a better opportunity.

Lincoln wholeheartedly devoted himself to the tasks that were set before him. Because he showed himself faithful with what little he had, he was soon given more (Luke 19:17). Having landed the first steamboat upon Springfield's busy shore earned him the smallest bit of fame and respect that he faithfully nurtured all the way to the presidency.

At each juncture, Lincoln applied maximum effort to grow and learn. To Lincoln, there was no excuse for idleness. Once, when his stepbrother asked to borrow money (as he often did),

Abe reproved him sharply, saying, "You are not lazy, and still you are an idler. I doubt whether since I saw you, you have done a good whole day's work. . . . This habit of uselessly wasting time is the whole difficulty; and it is vastly important to you, and still more to your children that you should break this habit." When asked by a law student how to succeed, he simply replied, "Work, work, work is the main thing."

Lincoln found satisfaction in doing a job well. Yet, at the same time, he understood the difficulty of putting one's heart into something that is not inspiring. Regarding the incentive to work, he made the following observation:

> Every man is proud of what he does well, and no man is proud of what he does not do well. With the former, his heart is in his work; and he will do twice as much of it with less fatigue. The latter performs a little imperfectly, looks at it in disgust, turns from it, and imagines himself exceedingly tired.

Concerning the issue of slavery, Lincoln said he "was roused" as he had never been before. "He was moved by a moral earnestness that gave his words new power, and thrust him forward as a leader," writes Benjamin Platt Thomas in *"Lincoln's Humor" and Other Essays*. This emotionally charged issue propelled Lincoln with a purpose that surpassed his greatest weaknesses and outweighed his gravest self-doubts. He labored with a fervent passion that buoyed him through his most difficult struggles and persisted as if his life, and the lives of countless thousands, depended on it—and they did. Lincoln worked hard, knowing that if he faithfully put forth his best effort, God would return the favor. He once prayed, "I have done all I can, and now you must help."

All of us have been given a unique purpose that inspires us to take action. In spite of the degree of our gifting or our calling, we must work to achieve it. We must exercise and discipline and train ourselves. The apostle Paul compared our lives to athletes training for a race (1 Cor. 9:24–25) or a soldier preparing for a battle (Eph. 6:11–18), both of whom must continuously strengthen and hone their skills and abilities. Lincoln showed us how to work as if all depended on our effort, but to pray as if all depended on God.

> Whatever you do, work heartily, as for the Lord and not for men, knowing that from the Lord you will receive the inheritance as your reward. You are serving the Lord Christ.
>
> Colossians 3:23–24 ESV

24

LOVE YOUR ENEMIES

*A drop of honey catches more flies than a gallon of gall.
If you want to win a man to your cause, first convince
him you are his sincere friend.*

Abraham Lincoln

One of the most remarkable and memorable qualities of Lincoln's leadership style was his ability to make lasting friends of even his bitterest foes. Beginning with the appointment of his cabinet, Lincoln embraced his opponents. He either won them over as friends or, if not, continued to put their talents to the country's best use. He looked past personalities and focused on the strengths each person offered for the greatest good of everyone. Most of those who initially despised or resented Lincoln eventually came to admire him as he navigated his way through a monumental maze of adversaries and conflicts.

Lincoln assembled his cabinet largely of men who ran against him for president. William Seward, Salmon Chase, and Edward Bates had all vied for the chief executive position. All of these cabinet members had prestigious backgrounds and extensive political experience. None more so than William Seward, who was Lincoln's fiercest opponent—both throughout the campaign season and during the first few months as a member of the cabinet. Secretary of State Seward undermined Lincoln's authority, going behind his back and making threatening ultimatums, but Lincoln managed to hold his own with such grace and composure that even Seward eventually realized "the president is the best of us," and admitted "his magnanimity is almost superhuman."

Attorney General Bates, who also initially underestimated Lincoln, ultimately agreed with Seward's public praises that Lincoln was "the best and wisest man he [had] ever known."

Edwin Stanton had cruelly snubbed Lincoln several years earlier during a famous patent-infringement lawsuit. The trial, for which Lincoln had spent several months preparing, was moved from Chicago to Cincinnati. In Cincinnati, Stanton took over the case, ignoring Lincoln because he presumed he was a backward country lawyer. Even after Lincoln won the presidential election, Stanton spoke disdainfully of him. Despite Stanton's well-known opinions, Lincoln appointed him as his secretary of war. Like Seward, Stanton came to admire Lincoln and confessed, "No men were ever so deceived as we at Cincinnati." John Hay, Lincoln's private secretary, wrote to Stanton after the assassination: "Not everyone knows, as I do, how close you stood to our lost leader, how he loved you and trusted you, and how vain were all the efforts to shake that trust and confidence."

Lincoln's most ardent adversaries often became his staunchest supporters. Lincoln held out his hand of friendship to political opponents, newspaper critics, and even Confederate soldiers. British writer Edward Dicey wrote of meeting Lincoln, "I was introduced to the President as one of his enemies. 'I did not know I had any enemies,' was the answer; and I can still feel, as I write, the grip of that great boney hand held out to me in token of friendship." Thomas Kidd, a friend from Springfield, wrote, "Innocent to a fault himself, he would join hands with all in friendship, believing, as I have often heard him say, that the world would be a better place for all of us if suspicion was less cultivated as one of the characteristics of our nature." A close colleague, Joseph Gillespie, concurred that Mr. Lincoln "never manifested any bitter hatred towards his enemies. It was enough for him in a controversy to get the better of his adversary in argument without descending to personal abuse."

Lincoln never held a grudge. First Lady Mary Todd remembered her husband's advice when she spoke of the evil done to him by others: "Do good to those who hate you and turn their ill will to friendship." And that's what Lincoln attempted to do, especially with Salmon Chase, the most embittered member of his cabinet. Chase felt he should have been president and never let anyone forget it. "Even to comparative strangers he could not write without speaking slightingly of the President," wrote Lincoln's private secretaries John Nicolay and John Hay.

Yet, even after accepting Chase's fourth resignation and admitting that he knew "meaner things about Governor Chase than any of those men can tell me," Lincoln appointed him chief justice of the United States. "I should despise myself if I allowed personal differences to affect my judgment of his fitness," Lincoln told Congressman Augustus Frank. "I have scriptural authority for appointing him," Lincoln wryly added. "You remember that when the Lord was on Mount Sinai getting out a commission for Aaron [to Moses], that same Aaron was at the foot of the mountain making a false god for the people to worship. Yet Aaron got his commission, you know."

Of course, Seward, Stanton, and Chase were fellow Republicans and abolitionists. But how did Lincoln regard those who opposed him on the battlefield? What were his sentiments toward Confederate, slave-owning secessionists leading the rebellion against the Union? A Confederate colonel recalled Lincoln's visit to him in a makeshift army hospital:

> He halted beside my bed and held out his hand. I was lying on my back, my knees drawn up, my hands folded across my breast. Looking him in the face, as he stood with extended hand, "Mr. President," I said, "do you know to whom you offer your hand?" "I do not," he replied. "Well," said I, "you offer it to a Confederate colonel who has fought you as hard as he could for four years." "Well," said he, "I hope a Confederate colonel will not refuse me his hand." "No, sir," I replied, "I will not," and I clasped his hand in both of mine.

Unfortunately, many Christians today are not willing—let alone able—to conduct themselves in this manner even within their own churches. Too many folks are more interested in promoting themselves and eliminating their opposition than in promoting the greater good—let alone the love of Christ. If we followed in Lincoln's footsteps and reached across the great divide of differences that hinder us from achieving unity and peace, setting aside the minutiae of petty disagreements, what impact would it have within the body of Christ? And what impact would our actions have on the world around us? How would the world respond if we showed them a love like this?

> I, therefore, the prisoner of the Lord, beseech you to walk worthy of the calling with which you were called, with all lowliness and gentleness, with longsuffering, bearing with one another in love, endeavoring to keep the unity of the Spirit in the bond of peace.
>
> Ephesians 4:1–3

25

STAND FIRM

Stand firm. . . . Hold firm as with a chain of steel.

Abraham Lincoln

After Abraham Lincoln was elected president of the United States, before he was inaugurated, he faced two major decisions that would alter the course of the nation. The first decision was related to his stand on the issue of slavery, and the second reflected his determination to keep the country unified. Both were deep moral issues as far as Lincoln was concerned. Both required a great deal of moral clarity—and an uncompromising stance.

Soon after his election, Lincoln challenged what came to be known as the "Crittenden Compromise." Senator John J.

Crittenden of Kentucky concocted the proposed constitutional amendments and congressional resolutions. The plan stated that the federal government had no right to abolish slavery, to interfere with a state's—or new territory's—decision to allow slavery, or to regulate the interstate slave trade; it also stated that the federal government should be "responsible for compensating slave owners whose attempts to recover a fugitive slave were prevented by violence." Furthermore, all of the amendments included in the proposal should be "made unalterable by any future congressional action."

Lincoln urged Congress to "entertain no proposition for a compromise in regard to the extension of slavery," and to "prevent, as far as possible, any of our friends from demoralizing themselves, and our cause, by entertaining propositions for compromise of any sort on 'slavery extension,'" and to "have none of it. Stand firm. . . . Hold firm as with a chain of steel."

The president adamantly opposed the compromise, even when his inner circle urged him to consider it. Unity was at stake; already North Carolina had threatened to secede. Certainly averting a civil war was worth a compromise of some kind. But Lincoln was not a man of compromise, especially when it involved a plan that he felt had a "radical moral defect at its core," and when supporting it would require "total moral capitulation."

From the beginning to the end of his presidency Lincoln stood firm. Even before Lincoln took office, the first state passed an ordinance of secession. The *New York Herald* wrote, "The passage of the secession ordinance by the South Carolina Convention has instead of intimidating the President elect, only made him firmer and more decided in his views on the reckless and unjustifiable attempt to break up the Union." Lincoln famously declared, "You have no oath registered in Heaven to destroy the government, while I shall have the most solemn one to preserve, protect and defend it." The *New York Herald* added, "He will not swerve from the conscientious and rigorous fulfillment of what he considers his constitutional obligations."

He tirelessly urged his fellow Republican Party members to remain steadfast and resolute regarding their stand on slavery. He wrote strong letters, privately conversed with party leaders, and spoke out in the halls of Congress: "We have just carried an election on principles fairly stated to the people. Now we are told in advance, the government shall be broken up, unless we surrender to those we have beaten. . . . If we surrender, it is the end of us. They will repeat the experiment upon us *ad libitum*."

In *Lincoln's Melancholy* Joshua Wolf Shenk observed, "Lincoln repeatedly explained compromise on the essential issue of the election would set a fatal example. If the losers at the ballot forced the victors to yield on the central point, the result could hardly be called democracy." Lincoln asserted, "We must settle this question now, whether in a free government the minority have the right to break up the government whenever they choose."

Regarding his resolve to preserve the Union at all cost, Lincoln stated, "I expect to maintain this contest until successful, or till I die, or am conquered, or my term expires, or Congress or the country forsakes me." Responding to his decision for emancipation, Massachusetts senator Charles Sumner commented to Harriet Beecher Stowe, author of the politically charged classic *Uncle Tom's Cabin*, "It is hard to move him from a position once he has taken it." Speaking about the Emancipation Proclamation, Lincoln said that he "would rather die than take back a word."

Time and time again, Lincoln refused to budge on the issues he believed mattered most. His tenacious refusal to compromise on bottom-line, core values provides us with a model of how we can respond in similar situations.

Contemporary society tells us that we shouldn't take a firm stand on issues of morality. "To each his own," we hear. But what would America be like today if Lincoln had given in to that same attitude about slavery or secession? Lincoln once wrote:

> You may burn my body to ashes and scatter them to the winds of Heaven: you may drag my soul down to the regions of darkness and despair to be tormented forever; but you will never get me to support a measure which I believe to be wrong, although by doing so I may accomplish that which I believe to be right.

> It is for freedom that Christ has set us free. Stand firm, then, and do not let yourselves be burdened again by a yoke of slavery.
>
> Galatians 5:1 NIV

26

Fear God

Whereas, it is fit and becoming in all people, at all times, to acknowledge and revere the supreme government of God; to bow in humble submission to his chastisements; to confess and deplore their sins and transgressions, in the full conviction that the "fear of the Lord is the beginning of wisdom."

Abraham Lincoln

*I*f there is one thing each person could do to save our country—just one thing—it would be to "fear the Lord." The Bible tells us that the fear of the Lord is the beginning of wisdom (take time to look up Job 28:28; Ps. 111:10; Prov. 9:10; 15:33; Isa. 11:2; 33:6). But how do we fear the Lord? Lincoln continually reminded citizens of his country to remember the

Lord in both the wonderful and troubling events they experience in their daily lives. He issued proclamations urging the nation to give thanks to God and to repent of ungodliness and ingratitude. He set aside days for prayer and fasting, for repentance, and for thanksgiving.

Lincoln discerned that a nation without God is a nation in peril. Like the prophet Jeremiah, he was convinced that the potential demise of the Union, accompanied by immense suffering and bloodshed, was the result of national pride rooted in the abomination of slavery. According to Dr. George G. Fox, author of *Abraham Lincoln's Religion*, both Jeremiah and Lincoln "believed that peace would come only when those who strayed would return to the right path and repent of their misdeeds." On March 30, 1863, Lincoln declared a national day of prayer and fasting, claiming that the nation needed to humble itself before God:

> Intoxicated with unbroken success, we have become too self-sufficient to feel the necessity of redeeming and preserving grace, too proud to pray to the God who made us. It behooves us, then, to humble ourselves before the offended Power, to confess our national sins, and to pray for clemency and forgiveness. . . . I therefore designate the 30th day of April 1863, as a day of national humiliation, fasting, and prayer.

The president was not alone in his desire to appeal to his heavenly Father. Senator Harlan from Iowa suggested that Congress pass a resolution to set apart a day for national prayer and humiliation. The document indicates that the purpose of the National Fast Day would be to seek "Him for succour according to His appointed way, through Jesus Christ." Concurring with Congress, Lincoln "counseled personal and national repentance," according to William J. Wolf in *The Almost Chosen People*. Wolf adds that Lincoln argued "the Bible and the course of history showed the necessity for a nation to acknowledge God." He urged the people to "keep the day holy to the Lord."

> It is the duty of nations as well as of men to owe their dependence upon the overruling powers of God, to confess their sins and transgressions, in humble sorrow, yet with assured hope that genuine repentance will lead to mercy and pardon; and to recognize the sublime truth, announced in the Holy Scriptures and proven by all history, that those nations only are blessed whose God is the Lord.

Lincoln further declared that "the awful calamity of war, which now desolates the land, may be but a punishment inflicted upon us for our presumptuous sins to the needful end of our national reformation as a whole people." He accused the nation of forgetting God and falling prey to pride, foolish imagination, and the illusion of lordship. "When Lincoln charged the nation with forgetting its need for redemption," Wolf observes, "it was as though he had paraphrased Luther's statement that the essence of sin is the sinner's unwillingness to admit that he is a sinner."

Lincoln firmly believed that God would hear and honor the humble prayers of his people. He believed that God was merciful and would graciously forgive every confessed sin.

How do we as a nation and as individuals walk in unity and peace? How can we be sure God is on our side? A Southern newspaper widely publicized Lincoln's reply to a clergyman who expressed the hope that the "Lord was on our side." Lincoln responded, "I am not at all concerned about that, for I know that the Lord is always on the side of the right. But it is my constant anxiety and prayer that I and this nation should be on the Lord's side."

How can we be sure we are on the Lord's side? We can begin by fearing God. Next, we can acknowledge that we are sinners. We can despise our sin and pray that God will deliver us from it. Unfortunately, we no longer observe national days of prayer and fasting, but we do—if only once a year—remember to give thanks. After all, it was Lincoln who issued the Thanksgiving Proclamation in 1863, which set the precedent for a national holiday every November reminding us to be thankful.

In showing gratitude to God for his blessings, let's speak out against the sins of our nation, intercede on behalf of those who sin against us, and willingly repent of the sin in our own lives. Let's strive to join God's side for the sake of our nation, communities, and homes. Each one of us is responsible to submit to God, purify our heart before him, and *always* give him thanks.

> Therefore submit to God. Resist the devil and he will flee from you. Draw near to God and He will draw near to you. Cleanse your hands, you sinners; and purify your hearts, you double-minded. Lament and mourn and weep! Let your laughter be turned to mourning and your joy to gloom. Humble yourselves in the sight of the Lord, and He will lift you up.
>
> James 4:7–10

27

BE ENCOURAGED BY GOD'S WORD

*Let no feeling of discouragement prey upon you, and
in the end you are sure to succeed.*

Abraham Lincoln

In the early morning hours of July 21, 1861, the Union
army made its first advance on the Confederate forces
that had gathered only twenty-six miles from Washington,
DC. What looked like certain victory suddenly turned into a
demoralizing defeat for the unseasoned soldiers and generals. At midday the citizens of Washington were celebrating
victory, but by late afternoon they feared for their lives. The
North was completely dismayed by the unexpected turn of
events. "Today will be known as *Black Monday*. We are utterly

and disgracefully routed, beaten, whipped by secessionists," recorded Union diarist George Templeton Strong.

That fateful day became known as the Battle of Bull Run. At noon news of a complete Union victory had been telegraphed to Lincoln and his cabinet. Washingtonians were preparing picnic baskets to celebrate with the returning troops, and hundreds in the streets "cheered vehemently, and seemed fairly intoxicated with joy." Back at army headquarters, General Scott was taking a nap. At 4:30 p.m., when telegraph dispatches proclaimed that "the Union had achieved a glorious victory," Lincoln decided to take his usual carriage ride with Tad and Willie.

Lincoln relaxed in his carriage, believing that the tide of battle had turned. In the middle of the night the Union forces had begun their march toward Manassas, Virginia, where the Confederate army was encamped. But nine thousand fresh Confederate troops arrived late in the battle to drive back the exhausted Union soldiers, who had been up all night and fighting since dawn. Surprised by the waves of Confederate reinforcements, the dismayed and tired Union army broke rank, turned, and fled. Mayhem ensued as "an uncontrolled retreat toward Washington was further confused by the panicked flight of horrified spectators," writes Doris Kearns Goodwin in *Team of Rivals*. Goodwin quotes one observer who wrote, "Army wagons, sutlers' teams, and private carriages, choked the passage, tumbling against each other, amid clouds of dust, and sickening sights and sounds," adding that "Muskets and small arms were discarded along the way. Wounded soldiers pled for help. Horses, running free, exacerbated the human stampede."

The next dispatch to reach Washington read, "General Mc-Dowell's army in full retreat. . . . The day is lost. Save Washington and the remnants of the Army." When Lincoln received the news, "he listened in silence, without the slightest change of feature or expression, and walked away to army headquarters," observed his aides Nicolay and Hay. Lincoln remained with his cabinet until a telegram from McDowell confirmed the defeat. Reinforcements were dispatched to defend the Capitol, and Lincoln returned to the White House, where he watched the weary and injured soldiers plod through the streets. He didn't sleep that night but devised a new strategy for moving the army forward, along with a nine-step plan to assure that this would never happen again. Walt Whitman reflected on this day:

> If there were nothing else of Abraham Lincoln for history to stamp him with, it is enough to send him with his wreath to the memory of all future time, that he endured that hour, that day, bitterer than gall—indeed a crucifixion day—that it did not conquer him—that he unflinchingly stemmed it, and resolved to lift himself and the Union out of it.

In the days that followed, Lincoln visited the troops in various regiments to encourage and comfort them. He delivered a speech to the troops at Fort Corcoran under the command of Colonel William T. Sherman. It was "one of the neatest, best, and most feeling addresses," Sherman said, that he had ever heard. Although Lincoln commented on the lost battle, he stressed "the high duties that still devolved on us, and the brighter days yet to come."

Where did Lincoln's steady hope and depth of courage come from? Mary Todd's seamstress, Elizabeth Keckley, who lived with the Lincolns, records in *Behind the Scenes* what she witnessed Lincoln do on one troubling day. He entered the room where she was fitting a dress for Mary and threw himself onto the full-length sofa, covering his face with his hands. "A complete picture of dejection," she writes. Mary asked him where he had been, and he abruptly replied, "The War Department." "Any news?" "Yes, plenty of news, but no good news. It is dark, dark everywhere," he answered. Keckley records Lincoln's ensuing actions:

> He reached forth one of his long arms and took a small Bible from a stand near the head of the sofa, opened the pages of the Holy Book, and soon was absorbed in reading them. A quarter of an hour passed and on glancing at the sofa the face of the President seemed cheerful. The dejected look was gone, and the countenance was lighted up with new resolution and hope. The change was so marked that I could not wonder at it. . . . He read with Christian eagerness, and courage and the hope he derived from the inspired pages made him a new man.

The Word of God strengthened and encouraged Lincoln. It made him a "new man" so that he was able to encourage others. He received a greater—more resilient—hope from reading the Bible, and this gave him the uncommon ability to resist discouragement regardless of the circumstances.

When faced with sudden failure or loss, he quickly turned the tables to encourage himself by encouraging those around him. He read Scripture, found solutions, made changes, and took action. The devastating defeat of battle and the loss of thousands of lives may not rest on our shoulders, but we can apply the same principles in our daily lives. We can overcome the gravest situation by turning to God's Word and staying in his presence.

> Be of good courage, and let us be strong for our people
> and for the cities of our God. And may the LORD do
> what is good in His sight.
>
> 2 Samuel 10:12

28

STAY FOCUSED

No small matter should divert us from our great purpose . . . do not let your minds be carried off from the great work we have before us.

Abraham Lincoln

All too often, trivial matters distract us from what is truly important. Criticism, fatigue, nerves, or depression can divert our attention. Sometimes a comment by someone we respect will convince us to stray from plans. But leaders follow their priorities and refuse to be dissuaded from their purpose. Neither people nor problems get in their way or cause them to lose their focus. They absorb themselves in their mission with great deliberation. With this same intensity, Lincoln prepared a speech that he would deliver in New York. Lincoln understood the importance of the task at hand and completely focused his efforts on making it a success.

Lincoln devoted an enormous amount of time and energy to the preparation of this address—more than for any other speech in his career. William Herndon recalled, "He searched through the dusty volumes of congressional proceedings in the State library, and dug deeply into political history. He was painstaking and thorough in the study of his subject." The subject was the "single central vision" of the 175 speeches he had given leading up to this defining moment: slavery. Lincoln focused his sights on "the necessity of excluding slavery from the territories as the first step toward putting the institution on the path to ultimate extinction."

In February of 1860 he headed for New York to deliver the speech that would catapult him to the center of the national political stage. He arrived on a Saturday and discovered that the following Monday he would address an audience of fifteen hundred people in the Great Hall of the Cooper Institute instead of the congregation at Plymouth Church in Brooklyn. For months he had worked tirelessly researching, writing, and rewriting his notes; now what seemed like the whole world would hang on his every word.

Focused on the enormity of the task at hand, Lincoln evaded every social distraction. Invited to lunch in the home of newspaper editor Henry C. Bowen after Sunday morning's services, he paused in the doorway and begged his leave: "I will not go in. I am not going to make a failure at the Cooper Institute tomorrow night, if I can help it." After Bowen insisted, Lincoln countered, "It is on my mind all the time, and I cannot be persuaded to accept your hospitality at this time. Please excuse me and let me go to my room at the hotel, lock the door, and there think about my lecture." That's what he did, and the nation would never be the same.

"As Lincoln drew to the end [of his speech], the hall was so quiet that when he paused, one could hear the sizzle of the gas burners," writes biographer Joshua Wolf Shenk. Then, with a moving sincerity Lincoln urged his listeners to take a stand against slavery:

> Let us stand by our duty fearlessly and effectively. Let us be diverted by none of those sophistical contrivances . . . such as groping for some middle ground between right and wrong: vain as the search for a man who should be neither a living man nor a dead man. . . . Let us have faith that right makes might, and in that faith let us to the end dare to do our duty as we understand it.

The *New York Tribune* reported that Lincoln's speech was the "most convincing political argument ever made in this city," and added that "no man ever before made such an impression on his first appeal to a New York audience." Forty years later, the famed lawyer and diplomat Joseph H. Choate recalled, "When he spoke, he was transformed before us. His eye kindled, his voice rang, his face shone and seemed to light up the whole assembly as by electric flash. For an hour and more he held his audience in the hollow of his hand." Journalist Noah Brooks wrote of his own experience: "When I came out of the hall, my face glowing with an excitement and my frame all a quiver, a friend, with his eyes aglow, asked me what I thought of Abe Lincoln, the rail-splitter. I said, 'He's the greatest man since St. Paul.' And I think so yet." Mason Brayman, a Democrat from Springfield, wrote:

> The speech was masterly, and fully sustained throughout; indeed a triumph . . . he seized the strong points of the argument, and went straight through; not losing a link, not tripping, not wanting words, but speaking with studied precision and grammatical accuracy; and not even turning aside to tell a story, or provoke a mirth, which so often characterizes his more free and easy performance at home.

Lincoln's focus changed the course of the nation. He remained steadfast in his efforts to eradicate slavery and to fulfill the vision of the nation's forefathers when they declared that "all men are created equal." Great purpose requires great focus. Whatever the task, whatever the challenge, put your heart, mind, and soul into it. Just as loving God requires our whole hearts, so do our individual callings. Be deliberate, single-minded, and wholly focused in your pursuits, and, like Lincoln, you will change the world.

> Brethren, I count not myself to have apprehended: but this one thing I do, forgetting those things which are behind, and reaching forth unto those things which are before, I press toward the mark for the prize of the high calling of God in Christ Jesus.
>
> Philippians 3:13–14 KJV

29

CALL GOD BY NAME

Yet under all circumstances, trusting our Maker, and
through His wisdom and beneficence, to the great body
of people, we will not despair nor despond.

Abraham Lincoln

Abraham Lincoln understood the nature and character of God. To him, God was more than a mystical
force; rather, God was somebody he could call on for guidance
and direction. So when Lincoln prayed or talked about God,
he did so in a very personal way. He called God by specific
names, showing the depth and sincerity of his knowledge of
his Maker. Calling God by the titles used in the Bible is tre-
mendously powerful, not only as a form of worship, but also

as a way of stirring our own faith in everything the Great I Am encompasses.

In *Abraham Lincoln: The Christian* William Jackson Johnstone notes that "in referring to the Deity, Mr. Lincoln used no less than forty-nine designations." Johnstone observes, "This is very significant, revealing, as it does, the breadth of his thinking and showing how full was his conception of God and His attributes." Likewise, we should recognize the vast nature of God. God wants to help us in every circumstance. We should call out to him by name, according to his character as revealed in Scripture.

Certainly, a knowledge of God's attributes—in addition to acknowledging them at every opportunity—fed Lincoln's faith. He deliberately called God by the specific name that was most relevant for the occasion: Almighty Architect, Arm, Hand, Power, Ruler of Nations, Creator, Christ, Crucified One, Disposer, Author, Eternal God, Divine Majesty, Providence, Father of Mercies, God of Hosts, God of Nations, God of Battles, Governor, Judge, Jesus, Just, Maker, Master, Most High, Omniscient Mind, Ruler of the Universe, Higher Power, Heavenly Father, Holy Spirit, Lord, Savior, Son of God, Son of Mary, and Supreme Being.

For example, in a reply to a letter on January 5, 1863, Lincoln invoked the "gracious favor of the God of Nations upon the struggles our people are making for the preservation of their precious birthright of civil and religious liberty." In responding to a caller congratulating him on the "success of our arms" after he had signed the Emancipation Proclamation, Lincoln admitted, "I did it believing we never should be successful in the great struggle unless we obeyed the Lord's command."

On September 3, 1864, in Lincoln's fourth Special Thanksgiving Proclamation, he referred to "the signal success that Divine Providence has recently vouchsafed to the operations of the United States fleet and army in the harbor of Mobile," and asked that prayer be made for "blessings and comforts from the Father of Mercies to the sick, wounded, and prisoners, and to the orphans and widows of those who have fallen in the service of their country."

Lincoln's God was a God for all circumstances. God is so much more than Father; he is to us such a great deal more than Creator; and he has promised to be so much more to us than Redeemer. We should take our cue from Lincoln and tap into all the magnificent facets of God by studying the myriad of names by which he is called, and then use those names when we call out to him. We can rely on the faithfulness of the God of All Comfort, who is God with Us and our Ever Present Help in Trouble. David prayed to God in this way. Search the Psalms for the many names David used. And then call on God by name.

> At that time people first began to worship the Lord by name.
>
> Genesis 4:26 NLT

30

Have a Grateful Heart

*It is no pleasure to me to triumph over anyone, but
I give thanks to the Almighty for the evidences of the
people's resolution to stand by free government and
the right of humanity.*

Abraham Lincoln

Probably more than any other president, Lincoln had reason to be ambivalent, if not bitter, toward God. After all his losses, it is hard to believe that Lincoln could be so adamant about always giving thanks to his heavenly Father. Lincoln had many reasons at his disposal to be ungrateful. Yet he thanked God. He had a grateful heart, which marked him as the nation's wisest, most courageous, and most godly leader.

Lincoln issued more proclamations thanking God than any other president. After his first year in office, Lincoln issued a Proclamation Recommending Thanksgiving for Victories. On April 10, 1862, he "recommended to the people of the United States that . . . they especially acknowledge and render thanks to our Heavenly Father."

The following year, he designated a national day of thanksgiving "to render the homage due to the Divine Majesty for the wonderful things he has done in the nation's behalf." This proclamation gives us a glimpse into the attitude of Lincoln's heart: "It is . . . right to recognize and confess the presence of the Almighty Father, and the power of his hand equally in these triumphs and his sorrows."

This echoes a proclamation Lincoln made early in his presidency, when he declared, "It is fit and becoming in all people, at all times, to acknowledge and revere the supreme government of God." These statements reveal Lincoln's firm belief in God's ultimate control over every event, regardless of the hardships or circumstances. Because of Lincoln's equally firm belief in God's boundless mercy, his only response could be gratitude.

In the fall of 1863 he established a National Day of Thanksgiving to be celebrated in November, and every president since then has followed his lead. Although this national holiday has remained one of the most distinctive of American traditions, few people observe it in the manner Lincoln intended. Read closely the original proclamation Lincoln issued on October 3, 1863:

> The year that is drawing toward its close has been filled with the blessings of fruitful fields and healthful skies. These bounties

are so constantly enjoyed that we are prone to forget the source from which they come. No human counsel hath devised, nor hath any mortal hand worked out these great things. They are the gracious gift of the Most High God, who, while dealing with us in anger for our sins, hath nevertheless remembered mercy. It has seemed to me fit and proper that they should be *solemnly, reverently, and gratefully acknowledged as with one heart and one voice by the whole American people*. . . . And I recommend to them that, while offering up the ascriptions justly due to Him for such singular deliverances and blessings, they do also, *with humble penitence for our national perverseness and disobedience . . . fervently implore the interposition of the Almighty Hand to heal the wounds of the nation*. (Italics added.)

On May 9, 1864, when the war turned in favor of the North, Lincoln quickly issued a Recommendation of Thanksgiving. He began it by stating, "Enough is known of the army operations within that last five days to claim an especial gratitude to God." He went on to urge people to continue to pray for "what remains undone" and closed with an appeal that "all patriots . . . unite in common thanksgiving and prayer to Almighty God."

In October 1864 he renewed his Thanksgiving Day Proclamation, urging his fellow citizens to "reverently humble themselves in the dust, and from thence offer up penitent and fervent prayers to the great Disposer of events for a return of the inestimable blessings of peace, union, and harmony throughout the land." Thanksgiving Day was not originally set aside for celebration and overindulgence, but rather for people to humble themselves before "Almighty God, the beneficent

Creator and Ruler of the universe," and to intercede on behalf of the nation.

Lincoln regularly gave thanks to his Father in heaven. On election night, November 9, 1864, he received the applause of his supporters and delivered a speech in which he clearly acknowledged his gratitude to God:

> I am thankful to God for the approval of the people. But while deeply grateful for this mark of their confidence in me, if I know my heart, my gratitude is free from any taint of personal triumph. . . . It is no pleasure for me to triumph over anyone, but I give thanks to the Almighty for the evidences of the people's resolution to stand by free government and the right of humanity.

Lincoln provides a model for how to walk in gratitude before God. At all times, for all things, we can give thanks—in the privacy of our hearts and in our public spheres of influence. We should never forget who is the Giver of every blessing and the Father of all good things. Let's remember to be grateful, especially during the most difficult times. We can trust, like Lincoln, that God's higher purposes are being accomplished in our lives and that he will give us the grace and mercy we need. Why not take a moment right now to meditate on this passage and remember how God has blessed you?

> In everything give thanks; for this is the will of God in Christ Jesus for you.
>
> 1 Thessalonians 5:18

31

DON'T BE A HYPOCRITE

God did not place good and evil before man, telling him to make a choice. On the contrary, he did tell him there was one tree of the fruit of which he could not eat, upon pain of certain death.

Abraham Lincoln

*L*incoln despised hypocrisy. He loathed two-facedness and double standards. He believed that the truth was truth and that a house divided against itself cannot stand. As he began studying law, he realized that its foundation—its very core—was right versus wrong, with nothing in between. "But the [Emancipation] Proclamation, as law, either is valid, or is not valid," he wrote in a letter. "If it is not valid, it needs no retraction. If it is valid, it can not be retracted, any more than the dead can be brought to life."

Either slavery was right or it was wrong, and Lincoln believed it was wrong. He could not reconcile slavery with Scripture. During the Lincoln-Douglas debates of 1854 Lincoln boldly asserted, "Slavery is founded in the selfishness of man's nature; opposition to it is in the love of justice; these principles are an eternal antagonism, and when brought into collision so fiercely as slavery extension brings them, shocks and throes, and convulsions must ceaselessly follow." Ten years later, Lincoln wrote his thoughts for a delegation of Baptists:

> To read the Bible, as the word of God himself, that "In the sweat of thy face shalt thou eat bread," and to preach therefrom that, "In the sweat of other men's faces shalt thou eat bread," to my mind can scarcely be reconciled with honest sincerity. When those professedly holy men of the South met in prayer and devotion, and, in the name of Him who said, "as ye would all men should do unto you, do ye even so unto them," appealed to the Christian world to aid them in doing to a whole race of men, as they would have no man do unto themselves, to my thinking they contemned and insulted God and His church far more than did Satan when he tempted the Saviour with the Kingdoms of the earth. The devil's attempt was no more false, and far less hypocritical.

When the Kansas-Nebraska Act was passed in 1854, allowing new territories to decide for themselves if they were to be slave or free, Lincoln was provoked to write his old friend Joshua Speed. He called the bill not a law but "violence from the beginning. It was conceived in violence, passed in violence, and is maintained in violence." In *Lincoln's Melancholy* Joshua Wolf Shenk writes, "He seethed about the actions of the proslavery men in Kansas, who had passed a constitution that made it a hanging offense to aid an escaping slave, or even talk about the rights of black people." Lincoln recalled the story of Haman in the book of Esther, who was hung on the same gallows he had intended for the Jews. "If, like Haman, they should hang upon the gallows of their own building, I shall not be among the mourners for their fate."

The Kansas-Nebraska Act compelled Lincoln to run for Senate. When the 1858 Republican State Convention chose him as their candidate in opposition to Democrat Stephen Douglas, Lincoln delivered his famous "House Divided" speech. He borrowed the words of Jesus to describe the eventual result of a nation divided on the issue of slavery. "A house divided against itself cannot stand. I believe this government cannot endure permanently half slave and half free. I do not expect the Union to be dissolved—I do not expect the house to fall—but I do expect it will cease to be divided. It will become all one thing, or all the other."

Lincoln wanted freedom for all people. Slavery and the hypocrisy surrounding it deeply grieved him. "As a nation, we began by declaring that 'all men are created equal.' We now practically read it, 'all men are created equal, except negroes.' When the Know-Nothings get control, it will read, 'all men are created equal except negroes, and foreigners, and Catholics,'" he wrote to Speed. (Know-Nothings were a rising party of "nativists" who were threatened by the influx of immigrants, especially Irish Catholics.) Lincoln saw how eager people are to draw lines separating the "worthy" from the "unworthy," and he recognized that these distinctions are motivated by selfishness and fear.

Hypocrisy begins in the heart. It causes people to say one thing yet do another. We must clearly articulate what we believe and why. But before we can be true with others, we must be honest and forthright with ourselves. Standing for the truth begins with a healthy fear of God. David prayed in Psalm 86:11, "Teach me Your way, O Lord, that I may walk and live in Your truth; direct and unite my heart to fear and honor Your name" (AMP).

Lincoln's heart prompted his response to the Kansas-Nebraska Act: "Can we as Christian men, and strong and free ourselves, wield the sledge or hold the iron which is to manacle anew an already oppressed race? 'Woe unto them,' it is written, 'that decree unrighteous decrees and that write grievousness which they have prescribed.' Can we afford to sin any more deeply against human liberty?"

Unless we choose to fear God more than other human beings, we will be forever bound by worldly fears and selfishness that leave us prone to hypocrisy.

> For let not that man suppose that he will receive anything from the Lord; he is a double-minded man, unstable in all his ways.
>
> James 1:7–8

32

WASH PEOPLE'S FEET

Unless the spirit and loyalty of the soldiers are kept up and encouraged in every way, the country is to suffer immeasurably before these troubles are disposed of.

Abraham Lincoln

Nowhere else do we see more clearly the extent of Lincoln's compassion than in the way he reached out to the Union soldiers. He appreciated each one and went to great lengths to show it. He was famous for spending time with the troops, listening to their problems, giving advice, and getting to know them. After spending many hours with them—a total of forty-two days in the field—he became known as the "common recruit's best friend." They called him Uncle Abe and Father

Abraham. He intentionally made himself visibly supportive, once standing for five straight hours to wave at thirty thousand troops passing through the streets of Washington.

Although he had negligible military experience and no experience as a military leader, he understood human nature. "It was precisely because of Lincoln's inability to be anything but himself that he became a successful commander in chief, judged by many historians to be the greatest of them all," writes Elizabeth Smith Brownstein in *Lincoln's Other White House*.

From Lincoln's brief experience in 1832 as a volunteer in the Black Hawk War, he understood the necessity of decent provisions and reliable pay. He advocated on behalf of soldiers at every opportunity and felt deeply their hardships and pain. Lincoln biographer Ida Tarbell wrote of his experience, "The President did not escape the sight of the wounded. . . . As he drove home after a harrowing day at the White House, the President frequently looked from his carriage upon the very beds of wounded soldiers." Brownstein adds, "If he happened upon an ambulance train on his way out to the home, he would ride along for some time, talking with the wounded. All of this, of course, tore Lincoln to pieces."

When any soldier needed help, Lincoln offered it. Two brothers went straight to Lincoln to appeal for help when their Confederate brother-in-law fell ill in a Union prison camp. He had been denied parole, so Lincoln immediately sent orders that he be released.

Lincoln was equally sympathetic to the injured enemy soldiers convalescing in the growing sprawl of makeshift hospitals in Washington. He regularly visited them, shaking their hands and offering a reassuring word. In June of 1863 the *Chicago Tribune* published an article lauding Lincoln as a great military strategist. The *Tribune* suggested he take command of the army, but then commented, "Our only apprehension would be that, just at the moment of victory, his kindness of heart would impel him to call a halt, lest the enemy should get hurt."

The greatest leaders are those who most appreciate the individuals who serve them. When it came to his soldiers, Lincoln embodied the Golden Rule. He felt their circumstances and was determined to do for them what he would want them to do for him. As a result, he won their trust and allegiance. They fully understood that he would do anything for them, and in turn they gave their lives for him.

> Sitting down, Jesus called the Twelve and said, "If anyone wants to be first, he must be the very last, and the servant of all."
>
> Mark 9:35 NIV

33

RECOGNIZE GOD IS SOVEREIGN

*Men are flattered by being shown there has been a
difference of the purposes of the Almighty and them.
To deny it, however, in this case, is to deny there is a
God governing the world.*

Abraham Lincoln

*I*t's easy to say that God is sovereign and in control when
we're happy, but it's much more difficult when things
don't go our way, or worse, when life appears to be spinning
out of control. In the midst of the war the going got very tough
for Lincoln. He felt overwhelmed by the tens of thousands
of casualties, a country torn apart, criticism from all sides,
betrayal from within his own party, and the death of a son.
Throughout 1864 and 1865 Lincoln desperately sought God for

direction. Instead of looking outward or inward, he meditated on the meaning of God's sovereignty.

In a telling letter he wrote to Quaker activist Eliza Gurney in the fall of 1864, he asserted:

> The purposes of the Almighty are perfect, and must prevail, though we erring mortals may fail to accurately perceive them in advance. We hoped for a happy termination of this terrible war before this; but God knows best, and has ruled otherwise. We shall yet acknowledge His wisdom, and our own error therein. Meanwhile, we must work earnestly in the best light He gives us, trusting that so working still conduces to the great ends He ordains. Surely He intends some great good to follow this mighty convulsion.

"Lincoln's preoccupation with the issue of God's will and the providential meaning of the nation's calamitous ordeal is particularly evident throughout the last year of his life," writes Douglas L. Wilson in *Lincoln's Sword*. Wilson traces the emerging theme of God's sovereignty in Lincoln's letters and speeches as he wrestled with the ongoing war. "When the war began, three years ago, neither party, nor any man, expected it would last till now. Each looked for the end, in some way, long ere today," he remarked in a speech in 1864. "Neither did any anticipate that domestic slavery would be much affected by the war. But here we are; the war has not ended, and slavery has been much affected. . . . So true is it that man proposes, and God disposes."

In an unfinished meditation found after Lincoln's death, we get a sense of how intensely he grappled with God's purpose regarding the ongoing war. "It is penned in the awful sincerity of a perfectly honest soul trying to bring itself into closer communion with his Maker," write Nicolay and Hay in *Abraham Lincoln: A History*. Lincoln wrote:

> The will of God prevails. In great contests each party claims to act in accordance with the will of God. Both may be, and one must be, wrong. God cannot be for and against the same thing at the same time. In the present civil war it is quite possible that God's purpose is something different from the purposes of either party—and yet the human instrumentalities working just as they do, are of the best adaptation to effect His purpose. . . . God wills this contest, and wills that it shall not end yet. By His mere great power on the minds of the now contestants, He could either have saved or destroyed the Union without a human contest. Yet the contest began. And having begun, He could give final victory to either side any day. Yet the contest proceeds.

In the summer of 1864 when Lincoln heard his presidential guard lamenting that they were not on the front lines where the action was, Lincoln told them this simple story: "You boys remind me of a farmer friend of mine in Illinois, who said he could never understand why the Lord put the curl in a pig's tail. It never seemed to him to be either useful or ornamental, but he reckoned the Almighty knew what he was doing when he put it there." In other words, notes Wilson in *Lincoln's Sword*, "Just because we can't understand the purpose of things, however insignificant, doesn't mean that there is none."

We must constantly remind ourselves, even as wise Solomon did, that "to everything there is a season, and a time for every matter or purpose under heaven" (Eccles. 3:1 AMP). When it seems from our temporal standpoint that all is lost, remember that God works from an eternal perspective and that he does everything for our good (Rom. 8:28). It might not seem as if things are good, but God is good, and he is still on the job, still paying attention, still in control.

> The LORD of hosts has sworn, saying,
> "Surely, as I have thought, so it shall come to pass,
> And as I have purposed, so it shall stand."
>
> Isaiah 14:24

34

RENEW YOUR SPIRIT

*Let us renew our trust in God and go forward without
fear and with manly hearts.*

Abraham Lincoln

*L*ike many of us, Lincoln burned the candle at both
ends. He worked tirelessly from daybreak until late in
the night, sometimes receiving visitors at midnight. He rarely
turned people away. Still, he managed a quarreling cabinet, a
devastating war, incompetent generals, the constant onslaught
of officeseekers, and the never-ending requests of common
citizens. Stacks of court-martial documents awaited his signature daily, piles of correspondence required his attention, and
lines of visitors perpetually waited for an audience.

"This poor President!" wrote William Russell, a correspondent for *The Times* of London. "He is to be pitied . . . trying with all his might to understand strategy, naval warfare, big guns, the movements of troops, military maps, reconnaissances, occupations, internal and exterior lines, and all the technical details of the art of slaying." Russell added, "He runs from one house to another, armed with plans, reports, recommendations, sometimes good-humored, never angry, occasionally dejected, and always a little fussy."

In a memorial essay, political and military strategist Carl Schurz enumerated some of the other obstacles Lincoln faced: "An empty treasury, departments honeycombed with disloyalty, cries for peace at any price . . . and a Europe hoping to see the United States fall apart." Yet twice a week Lincoln opened his office door to the public. Throngs of visitors began lining up at dawn to see him, with the lines stretching around the building and crowding every hall and corridor. "I feel," wrote Lincoln, "though the tax on my time is heavy—no hours of my day are better employed than those which thus bring me again within the direct contact and atmosphere of the average of our whole people."

Lincoln worked himself to the point of exhaustion and often illness. "If to be the head of Hell is as hard as what I have to undergo here, I could find it in my heart to pity Satan himself," he once told a friend. One observer wrote, "There were moments when his face was the picture of indescribable weariness and despair." And then in February of 1862 his beloved son Willie died after a long and feverish battle with typhoid. The need for rest was great.

By June of 1862 the Lincolns had moved to the large estate three miles north of the city known as the Soldiers' Home, resting on nearly 300 hilly acres. "It was beautiful," wrote Mary. Established in the 1850s as a retirement community for disabled veterans, it included several spacious cottages and a large dormitory that could house 150 boarders. The Lincolns occupied a two-story brick house known as the Anderson Cottage.

The Lincoln family stayed at the Soldiers' Home from June to November 1862, and they returned in 1863 and 1864. Lincoln rode his horse three miles to the White House every morning and left the White House around four or five o'clock every afternoon. "We are truly delighted with this retreat," wrote Mary to a friend. "The drives and walks around here are delightful, and each day brings its visitors. . . . We consider it a 'pleasant time' for us." Historian Matthew Pinsker records that the soldiers assigned to Lincoln's security detail "helped him recreate some of the spirit of fraternity that he had once enjoyed as a younger politician and circuit-riding attorney in Illinois."

"The Soldiers' Home was . . . an obvious retreat from the miseries and dangers of living in the White House," writes Brownstein. He then quotes a telling line from one of Mary's letters, "When we are in sorrow, quiet is very necessary to us." Though it wasn't always quiet, Lincoln made time for renewal at Anderson Cottage that could not be found at the White House.

"The tycoon is in fine whack," John Hay wrote of Lincoln in August of 1863. "I have rarely seen him more serene and busy. He is managing this war, the draft, foreign relations, and planning a reconstruction of the Union all at once." The bit of repose Lincoln could capture at the Soldiers' Home, and certainly the bit of fresh air, was necessary for him to continue leading with clear mind and strong body.

We all must guard ourselves against becoming too busy, too stressed, and too tired. We need rest as much as we need food, water, and air. We all need a quiet place to think, reflect, and pray. Without a quiet retreat, we cannot stay healthy, and we greatly diminish our usefulness to God.

> There remains therefore a rest for the people of God. For he who has entered His rest has himself also ceased from his works as God did from His. Let us therefore be diligent to enter that rest, lest anyone fall according to the same example of disobedience.
>
> Hebrews 4:9–11

35

FEED YOUR SOUL

*And I do hereby request all the People to abstain from
their ordinary secular pursuits, and to unite, at their
several places of public worship and their respective
homes, in keeping the day holy to the Lord, and devoted
to the humble discharge of the religious duties proper
to that solemn occasion.*

Abraham Lincoln

Abraham Lincoln nurtured his soul, much as he cultivated his mind and his body. Always learning and striving to improve, he fed his soul by reading the Bible, by praying, and by fellowshipping with others. In *Faith and the Presidency* historian Gary Scott Smith reports that "As an adult, Lincoln's church attendance was sporadic until 1850, when his son Eddie died at age three. From then until early 1861, Lincoln worshipped regularly at the First Presbyterian Church in Springfield." After Lincoln was elected president, Smith writes, "The prairie politician rented a pew at New York Avenue Presbyterian Church in Washington and faithfully attended services there." Although he never officially became a member of that church, he was one of its most faithful attendees.

Lincoln loved to hear the Word preached and to discuss Scripture with pastors. On one occasion, recalled Colonel Jacques, an army veteran turned pastor, Lincoln sent a little boy over to the parsonage to find out if he would be preaching. Jacques said, "You go back and tell Mr. Lincoln that if he will come to church he will see whether I am going to preach or not." The boy hesitantly replied, "Mr. Lincoln told me he would give me a quarter if I would find out whether you are going to preach." Jacques reported, "I did not want to rob the little fellow of his income, so I told him to tell Mr. Lincoln I was going to preach."

The church was packed that Sunday morning, so Lincoln was forced to sit on the altar. Jacques preached about the words of Jesus in John 3:7, "Ye must be born again" (KJV). "I noticed that Mr. Lincoln appeared to be deeply interested in the sermon," Jacques recalled. A few days later Lincoln visited him, "impressed with my remarks," and to discuss the subject further. "I invited him in, and my wife and I talked and prayed with him for hours. Now, I have seen persons converted; I have seen hundreds brought to Christ, and if ever a person was converted, Abraham Lincoln was converted that night in my house. He never joined my church, but I will always believe that since that night, Abraham Lincoln lived and died a Christian gentleman."

Despite Lincoln's reluctance to join a church, "Few American statesmen have cited or alluded to the Bible in public addresses as much as Lincoln," writes Smith. Carl Sandburg noted that Lincoln "read the Bible closely, knew it from cover to cover." Lincoln's private secretary John Nicolay declared, "He had great faith in [the Bible]." One of his bodyguards disclosed that he read at least one or two chapters from the Bible each morning. Lincoln fed his soul with the Word of God. He said that it "is the best book God has given to man. All the good from the Savior of the world is communicated in this Book." His son Robert remembered, "In the later years of his life, he always had a Bible . . . very near him," and it comforted him "at all times."

Not only did Lincoln regularly attend church, pray, and read the Bible, but he also enjoyed the fellowship—as well as the counsel—of church leaders. Edgar DeWitt Jones in *Lincoln and the Preachers* records that "It is likely that Abraham Lincoln had met and heard [Bishop] Matthew Simpson before the terrible war broke devastatingly over the nation." Jones includes a remark by Simpson's biographer, Dr. Crooks: "Conferences between them [Lincoln and Simpson] took place in Springfield, Mr. Lincoln's home, during the winter of 1860–61. While the war lasted the Bishop was often invited to come to Washington for consultations with the President and Mr. Stanton."

The Rev. Dr. Thomas Bowman, who was chaplain of the United States Senate during the later part of the war, observed:

It was well known that the President occasionally sent for the Bishop in order to procure information about the affairs of the nation. The President said in substance, "Bishop Simpson is a wise and thoughtful man. He travels extensively over the country and sees things as they are. He has no axe to grind, and therefore I can depend upon him for such information as I need."

Lincoln sought counsel from the great men of faith he respected. And rather than relying solely on his personal study of the Bible, he eagerly gleaned from the expositions he heard from the pulpit. Many have remarked how intently he listened to a sermon. When Lincoln was sitting with the congregation during one of Henry Ward Beecher's sermons, one of the ushers observed: "Mr. Lincoln's body swayed forward, his lips parted, and he seemed at length entirely unconscious of his surroundings—frequently giving vent to his satisfaction, at a well-put point or illustration."

Lincoln fed his soul. He nourished himself by reading the Word and hearing it preached, as well as conversing with people of faith, both lay and clergy. He regularly attended church and joyfully joined in fellowship with other believers. He did not neglect his soul, and neither should we!

> And let us consider one another in order to stir up love and good works, not forsaking the assembling of ourselves together, as is the manner of some, but exhorting one another, and so much the more as you see the Day approaching.
>
> Hebrews 10:24–25

36

IGNORE YOUR CRITICS

If I care to listen to every criticism, let alone act on them, then this shop may as well be closed for all other businesses. I have learned to do my best, and if the end result is good then I do not care for any criticism, but if the end result is not good, then even the praise of ten angels would not make the difference.

Abraham Lincoln

*P*erhaps more than any other president, Lincoln *knew* criticism. He was criticized for his physical appearance, his clothes, his lack of education and experience, and his lowly upbringing. Today Lincoln is revered, but in his own time many people despised him and the decisions he made as president. But Lincoln understood the adage "ignore your critics, and they'll go away." He didn't listen to critics or dwell on their negative comments. This lesson is as important for us as it was for him. When we encounter criticism, the worst thing we can do is to let it deter us from reaching our goals and fulfilling our dreams. Listening to criticism only serves to weaken our faith and diminish our enthusiasm.

Soon after he was elected president, Lincoln was resoundingly criticized by the press. Newspaper writers gave the newly elected president an ugly assortment of names. They called him "Abe the Rail-splitter," an "ape," and a "baboon." Early Lincoln biographer C. C. Coffin writes, "A few weeks after the inauguration a poem entitled 'The Royal Ape' was published in Richmond. Women were horrified that such a low-born man had just occupied the White House." Coffin tells of one such lady who saw Lincoln in a hotel parlor before his inauguration. "Why Mr. Lincoln, you look, act, and speak like a kind, good-hearted, generous man!" she told him. "Did you expect a savage?" Lincoln asked. "Certainly I did, or something worse. But I am glad that I have met you." Afterward she said to her friends, "That terrible monster, Lincoln; and instead of being a monster he is a gentleman and I mean to attend his first reception." This was not an unusual occurrence for Lincoln. He was often laughed at and scorned. But he moved forward with confidence, never allowing the criticism to lower his self-confidence.

Although Lincoln was courteous and well-spoken, people criticized his demeanor and his awkwardness. In 1855 Lincoln was hired to assist in representing a significant patent case with Stanton, Harding, and Watson, a famous law firm from the East. When the trial was relocated from Illinois to Ohio, the partners decided that they no longer needed Lincoln, because "the mere sight of him might jeopardize the case," as one historian put it. Stanton refused to associate with "such a damned, gawky, long-armed ape as that." However, they failed to communicate this to Lincoln. Instead, Lincoln stayed on the case, and he won the esteem of the law partners with his cunning arguments and his eloquence in the courtroom.

In 1846 Lincoln ran against Peter Cartwright for Congress. Cartwright was an early American hellfire-and-brimstone preacher, renowned for baptizing twelve thousand people and helping start the Second Great Awakening. Cartwright criticized Lincoln for not responding to his invitation to come forward during an altar call and called Lincoln an "infidel." Lincoln's preference was to ignore Cartwright's condemnation. But upon the advice of friends, Lincoln wrote a very short letter to his constituents responding to the accusation of being "an open scoffer of Christianity," and then quickly put the matter behind him:

> That I am not a member of any Christian Church, is true; but I have never denied the truth of the Scriptures; and I have never spoken with intentional disrespect of religion in general, or of any denomination of Christians in particular.

Lincoln prevailed over Cartwright—despite Cartwright's huge popularity—by focusing on his goals and ignoring Cartwright's claims.

Throughout his presidency, Lincoln continued to battle fierce condemnation. His opponents repeatedly criticized him

WALKING WITH LINCOLN

for his cabinet appointments, for the length of the war, for not freeing the slaves soon enough, and then later for freeing them. He faced criticism on every side. "Violent criticism, attacks, and denunciations, coming either from radicals or conservatives, rarely ruffled the President," writes J. B. McClure in his classic compilation *Anecdotes and Stories of Abraham Lincoln*. It must have been in connection with something of this kind, that he once told a friend this story:

> "Some years ago" said he, "a couple of 'emigrants,' fresh from the 'Emerald Isle,' seeking labor, were making their way toward the West. Coming suddenly one evening upon a pond of water, they were greeted with a grand chorus of bull-frogs—a kind of music they had never before heard. 'B-a-u-m!'—'B-a-u-m!'
>
> "Overcome with terror, they clutched their 'shillelahs,' and crept cautiously forward, straining their eyes in every direction to catch a glimpse of the enemy; but he was not to be found!
>
> "At last a happy idea seized the foremost one—he sprang to his companion and exclaimed, 'And sure, Jamie! It is my opinion it's nothing but a noise!' "

What if people called you an ape? What if, when you awoke in the morning and opened the newspaper, you saw your decisions reviled and despised? If you plan on doing anything significant with your life, you should also plan on having critics. The best way to silence them is to ignore them and move on toward the goal! Don't listen to criticism for doing what you know is right. Don't let critics weigh you down with guilt or rob you of your confidence. Remember, "It's nothing but a noise!"

The LORD is on my side;
    I will not fear.
    What can man do to me?
The LORD is for me among those who help me;
    Therefore I shall see my desire on those who hate
      me.
It is better to trust in the LORD
    Than to put confidence in man.

                          Psalm 118:6–8

37

BE GOD'S INSTRUMENT

*In the very responsible position in which I happen to
be placed, being a humble instrument in the hands
of our Heavenly Father, as I am, and as we all are, to
work out his just purposes.*

Abraham Lincoln

Too often we work hard and strive under our own power,
hoping to make a difference for the kingdom of God,
but Lincoln simply offered up his life to be used as God saw fit.
He didn't take credit for his own successes; instead, he pointed
to his heavenly Father. He humbly submitted himself to God,
and in turn God lifted him up and used him to steer the nation
through its most turbulent period in history. Lincoln's willingness to yield to the sovereign purposes of God, who he was

convinced had preordained the greatest good, is evident in a letter he wrote to the Quaker abolitionist Eliza Gurney:

> I have desired that all my works and acts may be according to His will, and that it might be so, I have sought His aid; but if, after endeavoring to do my best in the light which He affords me, I find my efforts fail, I must believe that for some purpose unknown to me, He wills it otherwise. If I had had my way, this war would never have been commenced. If I had been allowed my way, this war would have ended before this; but we find it still continues, and we must believe that He permits it for some wise purpose of His own, mysterious and unknown to us; and though with our limited understandings we may not be able to comprehend it, yet we cannot but believe that He who made the world still governs it.

Lincoln did not necessarily feel equipped or prepared. He was a rough and unusual instrument for God to use in such a great role. And although he often felt more like a rusty gardening tool operating among highly polished silverware, his heart was pliable and willing to be used, and that made him a very fine instrument in the hands of God. "God selects his own instruments," he wrote to his friend James Gilmore, "and sometimes they are queer ones; for instance, He chose me to steer the ship through a great crisis."

Lincoln was certainly an improbable leader. But remember the shepherd boy God chose to be king over Israel (David), or the betrothed of a carpenter he chose to give birth to the Messiah (Mary). Why does God deliberately choose improbable people to accomplish his purposes? Perhaps because he wants to make clear that the power lies in him, not in us. In the same way, he often uses broken people—people like Lincoln. The future president grew up in the humblest of beginnings, lost what little he treasured in life, and yet was seemingly willing to forfeit nearly everything to obey God. He refused to promote himself, readily giving honor where honor was due. "Don't kneel to me," he told a group of African-Americans in Richmond after it was liberated. "You must kneel to God only, and thank Him. . . . I am but God's humble instrument."

Lincoln introduced his good friend Joshua Speed to the woman who eventually became Speed's wife, Fanny, and was grateful to be useful in such a capacity. He also acknowledged that he was one instrument in a symphony of many who carried out God's will. "I believe God made me one of the instruments of bringing your Fanny and you together, which union I have no doubt He had foreordained," he later told Joshua.

Let God use you. Be God's instrument and strive to serve him only. "I shall be most happy indeed," Lincoln declared in a speech to the New Jersey Senate on February 21, 1861, "if I shall be a humble instrument in the hands of the Almighty." Make that goal your ultimate joy as well. The world will be blessed as a result.

> Therefore if anyone cleanses himself from the latter, he will be a vessel for honor, sanctified and useful for the Master, prepared for every good work.
>
> 2 Timothy 2:21

38

Be Patient

All we want is time, patience, and a reliance on a God who has never forsaken this people.

Abraham Lincoln

Although patience is valued and esteemed by nearly everyone, it is one of the most difficult virtues for most of us to practice. Because Lincoln lived with an exceptionally healthy fear of God, he was able to exercise an almost superhuman patience from early in his career. This quality made him an excellent lawyer and an even better statesman. He learned to trust in God's wisdom and wait for the "fullness of time" to make his move.

Lincoln understood the power of suffering with fortitude. Confident in God's sovereignty and his control over human history, Lincoln endured the evils he saw at work in the nation. He waited until the last possible moment to declare war on the South and patiently endured the ups and downs of the war until the ultimate victory was achieved. His patience was rooted in accepting God's sovereignty over all affairs—national and personal. Before his inauguration in February of 1861, Lincoln told the New York legislature, "If we have patience, if we restrain ourselves, if we allow ourselves not to run off in a passion, I still have confidence that the Almighty, the Maker of the Universe, will . . . bring us through this as He has through all the other difficulties of our country." He reminded his audience that "confidence in God" empowers human beings to be patient. From the outset, Lincoln tried to persuade the nation that God was in control.

Before the war began, Lincoln worked hard to end slavery and keep the country together without bloodshed. In an 1859 speech he stated, "We don't intend to be very impatient about it. We mean to be as deliberate and calm about it as it is possible to be." He begged the country to exercise patience by using ballots instead of bullets. "You can better succeed with the ballot," he said in 1855; "you can peaceably redeem the government and preserve the liberties of mankind through your votes and voice of moral influence." In an 1856 speech he counseled, "Let the legions of slavery use bullets; but let us wait patiently till November and fire ballots at them in return; and by that peaceful policy I believe we shall ultimately win." Lincoln hoped to avoid war, to keep the Union together, and to end slavery by waiting for the democratic process to prevail. He asked the country to be patient and to avoid violence at all cost. He was willing to wait for the citizens of America to peacefully resolve the issue. "There is no need for bloodshed . . . no necessity for it," he urged. "The government will not use force unless force is used against it." Despite strong opposition to slavery and to the secessionists who were already creating an army and forming their own government, Lincoln waited. "There will be no invasion, no using of force against the people anywhere," he proclaimed in his First Inaugural Address in 1861.

After the war began and progressed, he asked the people to again exercise patience. After three years of brutal bloodshed, he pointed once more to the sovereignty of God. He stated, "We accepted this war . . . for a worthy object, and the war will end when that object is attained. Under God, I hope it will never end until that time."

Lincoln patiently endured waves of opposition, criticism, threats, and even good-sounding advice while he stayed the course that God had placed him on. He did this because he was convinced that he was aligned with the will of God. That is the key. If we are to continue in patience and endure the trials set before us, we must be assured that God is on our side and confident that we are on his side. The best way to "keep in step with the Spirit" (see Gal. 5:25 NIV) is to be patient. When areas in your life seem to require superhuman patience, surrender them to the Lord, and the waiting that seemed impossible will become possible.

> Let patience have its perfect work, that you may be perfect and complete, lacking nothing.
>
> James 1:4

39

KEEP YOUR COOL

Be careful to give no offence, and keep cool under all circumstances.

Abraham Lincoln

*W*e must be calm and moderate. . . . We must not be led by excitement and passion to do that which our sober judgment would not approve in our cooler moments," Lincoln once said in a speech. He was already exhorting his listeners to "keep cool" as early as 1856. This quality served him well throughout his series of debates with Stephen Douglas in 1858 and when he entered the presidency in 1861 and became the nation's commander in chief. Lincoln continually exhorted those around him—and the nation as a whole—to "keep cool."

It was a phrase he used both in public and in private, and he worked hard to follow this advice in his own life.

Too often we lose our cool when confronted with people and situations that we cannot control. We lose our temper and say or do things we later regret. When we lose our cool, we often offend people, and our actions may result in destructive consequences.

Lincoln was not prone to anger or irritability. He maintained a calm and consistent demeanor, which proved to be an invaluable strength during times of incivility and short tempers. "If the great American people can only keep their temper on both sides of the line, the troubles will come to an end, and the question which now distracts the country will be settled," he advised his listeners in a speech in Pittsburgh on February 15, 1861. "Let the people on both sides keep their self-possession, and just as other clouds have cleared away in due time, so will the great nation continue to prosper as heretofore."

Lincoln could not afford to lose his composure, especially as the North suffered terrible losses and the war dragged on year after year. Even as the Confederates approached Washington, Lincoln urged the people to stay calm. "Let us be vigilant," he wrote to Thomas Swan in July of 1864, "but keep cool. I hope neither Baltimore nor Washington will be sacked." Only a calm preparedness could defend against such an attack, while panic would guarantee defeat.

Lincoln guarded his peace of mind by refusing to read the threatening letters and defamatory reports he received every day. "As a general rule," Lincoln said in his last public speech on April 11, 1865, "I abstain from reading the reports of attacks

171

upon myself, wishing not to be provoked by that to which I cannot properly offer an answer." In Lincoln's reply to a "cross letter" from Governor H. R. Gamble of Missouri, we can see how determined he was to protect his disposition: "My private secretary has just brought me a letter; says it is a very 'cross' one from you. . . . As I am trying to preserve my own temper by avoiding irritants so far as possible, I decline to read the cross letter." Perhaps we, too, would benefit by ignoring disagreeable email messages or other correspondence.

Take Lincoln's advice—don't be led by passion and excitement. Be calm, sober, and use sound reasoning. Of course, most of us know that losing our cool only leads to destruction and regret, but remembering this in the heat of battle is a challenge. Those critical moments present us with the opportunity to follow the advice of Proverbs 3:5: "Trust in the LORD with all your heart, and lean not on your own understanding." If we seek God's will and follow it, he will make our path straight and see us through every crisis.

> Be anxious for nothing, but in everything by prayer and supplication, with thanksgiving, let your requests be made known to God; and the peace of God, which surpasses all understanding, will guard your hearts and minds through Christ Jesus.
>
> Philippians 4:6–7

40

SHARE THE LOAD

*You are vigilant and self-reliant; and, pleased with
this I wish not to obtrude any constraints upon you. . . .
And now, with a brave army and a just cause, may
God sustain you.*

Abraham Lincoln

On April 30, 1864, a year before the end of the war, Lincoln spoke these words to General Ulysses S. Grant. Until March of that year, Lincoln issued many military orders directly from the White House. One after the other, his generals failed him. Lincoln grew weary of managing the entire war effort from his office, so when General Grant won important victories in Vicksburg and Chattanooga, Lincoln decided to delegate the entire direction of the war to Grant. He gave him full authority to maneuver as he thought best.

Like Moses, who heeded Jethro's advice to share the load, Lincoln decided he could no longer do everything. In Exodus 18, Moses's father-in-law told him that he was going to wear himself out if he continued to serve as the only judge. Jethro also urged him to appoint others to help him do the work. In the same way, Lincoln realized that delegating leadership is more effective than controlling leadership. He had confidence in Grant and was impressed by his humility and unassuming character. Like Lincoln, and unlike the other generals, Grant fully focused on the task at hand, refusing to be distracted by showmanship or status, and he felt the same urgency that Lincoln felt to once and for all crush the enemy.

"Nothing that I have done, or probably shall do, is to delay, hinder, or interfere with your work," Lincoln told Grant. "Let nothing that is transpiring change, hinder, or delay your military movements or plans." Through the last months of fighting, Lincoln continued to trust Grant's judgment. On March 13, 1865, as Grant approached Richmond, the Confederate capital, Lincoln reiterated, "I do not wish to modify anything I have heretofore said as to your having entire control."

Lincoln admitted that he could no longer issue military orders by himself. He deliberately sought to share his load with Grant. After he granted him the authority, he let go of the reins, and for the next eleven months Grant drove his Union forces south to Richmond, securing Lee's surrender on April 9, 1865. Victory was achieved at last.

Find people who can share your load—people you can trust to get the job done. Then allow them to do it. Let go, and give them authority, time, resources, and "mental space" to work it out. It will empower you and the people to whom you have delegated the job.

> And the keeper of the prison committed to Joseph's hand all the prisoners who were in the prison; whatever they did there, it was his doing. The keeper of the prison did not look into anything that was under Joseph's authority, because the LORD was with him; and whatever he did, the LORD made it prosper.
>
> Genesis 39:22–23

41

Have a Servant's Heart

Nearly all men can stand adversity, but if you want to test a man's character, give him power.

Abraham Lincoln

If a man's character was ever tested, it was Lincoln's. Although he wielded more power than any other person in the country, he continued to cultivate a deep sense of humility. His heart was fully directed by two primary motivations: serving God and serving his fellow citizens. Lincoln understood that the power at his disposal came not from himself or his efforts, but had been granted to him from above and by others. "Encompassed by vast difficulties as I am, nothing shall be wanting on my part, if sustained by God and the American people," he told an Ohio audience in 1861.

"I am, you know, only the servant of the people," Lincoln confessed to his friend James Gilmore. Lincoln sincerely felt accountable to his constituency. He opened his doors twice weekly to the public in order to listen to their concerns, suggestions, and complaints. As a public servant, he felt responsible and accountable to his fellow Americans—his power came from the people and was intended to serve the people. "I do say that in accepting the great trust entrusted to me, which I do with a determination to endeavor to prove worthy of it, I must rely upon you, upon the people of the whole country, for support," he told a New York gathering. And to longtime friend James Conkling he confided privately, "I freely acknowledge myself the servant of the people according to the bond of service—the United States Constitution—and that, as such, I am responsible to them."

Lincoln's humility enabled him to keep this perspective throughout his presidency. He was an outstanding facilitator, willing to do whatever was necessary to empower the people around him so they could fulfill their duties and accomplish the tasks at hand. General McClellan continually tested Lincoln's leadership and insulted him. The general fancied himself to be a great military leader and enjoyed hearing people call him "a young Napoleon." Lincoln gave him command of the great Army of the Potomac, mainly because public opinion affirmed his leadership. His performance, however, was less than sensational. Lincoln then commissioned him general-in-chief, hoping that this would propel him into action, but McClellan's habitual procrastination diluted his effectiveness.

One evening Lincoln and two of his staff members went to visit McClellan, only to learn that he was at a wedding. The three men sat down to wait, and an hour later the general arrived home. Without paying any attention to the president, McClellan walked upstairs and did not return. Half an hour later, Lincoln sent the servant to tell McClellan that the men were waiting. The servant came back reporting that McClellan had gone to bed. His associates were angry, but Lincoln merely stood up and led the way home. "This is no time to be making points of etiquette and personal dignity," the president explained. "I would hold McClellan's horse if he will only bring us success." This attitude of humility contributed to Lincoln's greatness as a man and as a president. He chose to prefer others above himself.

Harvey Lee Ross, who worked with Lincoln while he was postmaster in New Salem, noted Lincoln's heart of service. In *Lincoln's First Years in Illinois*, he describes Lincoln's willingness to help him with some land title paperwork by walking with him to see a judge after the judge had already gone home for the day. When they arrived at the house a mile outside of town, the judge's wife told them that he was in the field erecting a corncrib. Ross relates that Judge Thomas "fixed the papers" right there in the cornfield. But the significant part of this story is Ross's observation about Lincoln's assistance in helping the judge roll some logs:

> Now, there is something a little remarkable in the history of those two men who worked together rolling up those two logs.

It showed that the prominent men of that time were not too proud to engage in common labor. Judge Jesse B. Thomas, who was engaged at one end of the log, had served as representative in the Territorial Legislature of Illinois, had been twice elected to the United States Senate, once as a supreme judge, and as a member of the constitutional convention that framed the first constitution of Illinois, had done more and had exerted a greater influence toward making the State of Illinois a slave state than any other man. While the man at the other end of the log was Abraham Lincoln, who afterwards served in the Legislature, in Congress and as President of the United States, and who did more to banish slavery from the United States than any other man.

Oftentimes when given positions of power and authority, we forget that our tasks were created for the purpose of serving others. We forget that true power and authority come from humbly serving the people who serve us. Our influence makes us prideful and arrogant. We stop listening, we lack empathy, and we believe too strongly in our own opinions and views. Power corrupts most people, but Abraham Lincoln left us with an example of servant leadership. And so did another great leader, Jesus Christ. We would do well to follow their lead.

> If anyone desires to be first, he shall be last of all and servant of all.
>
> Mark 9:35

42

Pursue Not Riches

There is powerful temptation in money.

Abraham Lincoln

*Y*ou are pauperizing this court, Mr. Lincoln," chided Judge Davis. "You are ruining your fellows. Unless you quit this ridiculous policy we shall all have to go to farming!" Lincoln frustrated his fellow lawyers because he refused to accept a larger fee for his legal services than what he thought fair or what he felt a client could comfortably afford. Uninterested in amassing wealth, he was content with earning only enough to provide for his daily needs. Perhaps because he had endured great poverty for long seasons of his life, he was especially faithful in the smallest details regarding money. He was unfailingly honest in all his financial doings, and he was selflessly generous with his assets—including his time and professional services.

On one occasion, a client who owed him for his services experienced a financial hardship and soon afterward lost his hand. Lincoln promptly returned his note, saying, "If you had had the money I would not take it." Furthermore, if a fee was not paid, he did not believe in suing for it. According to his partner William Herndon, he would allow himself to be swindled rather than contesting a fee.

Lincoln grew up understanding the value of a dollar. On the frontier, where survival required sweat and toil, money had less value than a strong back and a good ax. Frontier people were self-sufficient and accustomed to hard work. Those values were deeply instilled in Lincoln. Even as a successful lawyer and politician, he chopped his own wood and tilled his own garden. Yet in his thriving law practice, his income averaged only two thousand dollars a year. "Lincoln's fees were as a rule smaller than his clients expected or his fellow lawyers approved of," writes Ida Tarbell in *The Life of Abraham Lincoln*. One client noted in amazement that Lincoln only charged him $3.50 for collecting nearly $600 in a successful lawsuit.

"Such charges were felt by the lawyers of the Eighth Circuit, with some reason, to be purely quixotic," writes Tarbell. "They protested and argued, but Lincoln went on serenely charging what he thought his services were worth." When a law partner collected a large fee for a case that the two had tried together, Lincoln refused to accept a cent of it until a portion had been refunded. It was in reaction to this that Judge Davis accused Lincoln of "pauperizing the court."

Lincoln continued his habit of returning funds he did not feel justified in keeping. While campaigning for the legislature, he received a contribution of $200 toward his personal expenses. At the end of the campaign, he handed his friend Joshua Speed $199.25, asking him to return it to the contributors. "I did not need the money," he told him. "I made the canvass on my own horse; my entertainment, being at the houses of friends, cost me nothing, and my only outlay was seventy-five cents for a barrel of cider which some farm-hands insisted I should treat them to." His actions are reminiscent of Jesus's words in Luke 16:9, "I tell you, use worldly wealth to gain friends for yourselves, so that when it is gone, you will be welcomed into eternal dwellings" (NIV).

Lincoln was not enamored by money. Davis noted that it did not seem to be one of the purposes of his life to accumulate a fortune; Lincoln felt that a house like his in Springfield and twenty thousand dollars, which he hoped to earn before his working days were over, were "all that a man ought to want." Like the apostle Paul, Lincoln learned to be content in the lowliest state, as well as in times of abundance. From a lowly farmhand, to a poor store clerk, to becoming president of the United States, Lincoln learned how to abound with true grace.

Today we face even greater pressures to gain wealth. Yet for Lincoln, money was simply a means to survive. This attitude offers us an important spiritual lesson: success and blessing followed Lincoln because he didn't follow after money. His generosity and honesty gained him stature in his community. Once he began obtaining wealth, he refused to allow it to divert him from his purpose. In Lincoln's position, it would have been easy to pursue money, but because he remained focused on his goals—which did not include getting rich—God blessed him with so much more.

> Do not wear yourself out to get rich;
>   have the wisdom to show restraint.
> Cast but a glance at riches, and they are gone,
>   for they will surely sprout wings
>   and fly off to the sky like an eagle.
>
> Proverbs 23:4–5 NIV

43

TAKE ACTION

He who does something at the head of a regiment will eclipse him who does nothing at the head of a hundred.

Abraham Lincoln

We can prepare and plan, but until we take action, our plans and preparations are for naught. Too often we fail to take action in our lives. Too often we conceive great ideas and grand plans, but then we procrastinate and never follow through. Perhaps our reluctance to bring our dreams to fruition results from the fear of failure or the insistence on perfection, or maybe our lives are simply too busy. But the procrastination that gives rise to such excuses quickly derails the dreams we once had. Lincoln despised procrastination. The delays, setbacks, and defeats resulting from his generals' failure to act continually frustrated him. He repeatedly urged them to take action.

"Now is the time for decision—for firm, persistent, resolute action," he declared in an 1856 speech. He never wavered from that sentiment. From the beginning of the war, Lincoln urged, "Do not delay a single regiment, but hasten everything forward." To General Buell he wrote in early 1862, "Delay is ruining us." Lincoln felt an extreme urgency about pursuing and defeating the enemy. With every delay, the enemy was able to reinforce and strengthen its position. "By delay the enemy will relatively gain upon you—that is, he will gain faster by fortifications and reinforcements than you can by reinforcements alone," he told General McClellan in April of 1862. He continued, "Once more let me tell you that it is indispensable to you that you strike a blow. . . . The country will not fail to note—is now noting—that the present hesitation to move upon an entrenched enemy is but the story of Manassas [the defeat at Bull Run] repeated. . . . You must act."

After a year of frustrating defeats and "near victories," Lincoln's persistent exhortations finally yielded a glimmer of hope and a potential turning point to the war in the first several days of July 1863. General Lee had made a bold advance into Pennsylvania at Gettysburg, where Union forces soon moved in to secure the town. Northern and Southern troops clashed in the streets and pushed the battle into the outlying fields. After two days of intense artillery fire, Lee's forces retreated after losing a third of their troops. With their backs to the rain-swollen, almost impassable Potomac River, the depleted Army of Northern Virginia was extremely vulnerable. Nevertheless, the Confederate troops secured a strong defensive position while General Meade organized another attack. As the crucial moments passed, General Lee and his vulnerable troops crossed the perilous river and regrouped, strengthened by thousands of fresh reinforcements.

Meade was criticized for not aggressively pursuing the Confederates during their retreat. Lincoln believed the general had lost an opportunity to end the war. "We had them within our grasp. We had only to stretch forth our hands and they were ours. And nothing I could say or do could make the Union army move," he told John Hay. To Meade he wrote, "Your golden opportunity is gone, and I am distressed immeasurably because of it." On July 21 he reiterated his frustration to General Oliver Howard:

> I was deeply mortified by the escape of Lee across the Potomac, because the substantial destruction of his army would have ended the war, and because I believed such destruction was perfectly easy—believed that General Meade and his noble army had expended all the skill, and toil, and blood, up to the ripe harvest, and then let the crop go to waste.

The war would continue to rage for almost two more years because Lincoln's generals failed to act at critical moments such as this. Thousands of lives were lost as a result.

Procrastination can lead to losses of epic proportions or, at the very least, to frustration and regret. We can learn from Lincoln's proactive approach to life. Don't delay; don't put off until tomorrow victories that can be won today. As Lincoln said, "Now is the time for decision—for firm, persistent, resolute action."

> What you have seen me do, make haste and do as I have done.
>
> Judges 9:48

44

Hold No Malice

I shall do nothing in malice. What I deal with is too vast for malicious dealings.

Abraham Lincoln

The word *malice* has fallen out of everyday use. In Lincoln's day, however, the word was quite common. Perhaps the nature of relationships between neighbors and states during the time of the Civil War prompted its greater prevalence. Or perhaps on the frontier, where common civility did not always prevail, there were ample reasons to act or react out of malice. During that time, the word was commonly employed as a legal term referring to a party's intention to injure or harm another person—often in retribution for a wrong. Today we might use the words *spite, vengeance, cruelty,* or *hatred.*

Lincoln often spoke of his determination to avoid harboring malice toward anyone and to avoid acting out of malice, especially toward the South. In his speeches he repeatedly exhorted the nation to do the same. In one speech, referring to the South, he stated, "I say this without malice in my heart toward those who have done otherwise." And on another occasion, he confessed, "I can only say that I have acted upon my best convictions, without selfishness or malice, and that by the help of God I shall continue to do so."

In his Second Inaugural Address, when Union forces were sweeping toward final victory, Lincoln spoke at length about the attitude the victors should have toward the vanquished. The president was deeply concerned that a pervasive bitterness and hatred between the North and the South would hinder the nation from healing. Although he ardently believed that slavery was a hateful and evil practice—a sin in the sight of God—he admitted that both North and South shared the burden of guilt. The "mighty scourge of war" was punishment on the entire country, which had so complacently allowed human bondage to flourish on its soil. With the permanent abolishment of slavery after the passage of the Thirteenth Amendment, the time had come for healing. Lincoln felt no malice, no hatred toward the Southern people who had taken up arms against the United States.

> With malice toward none; with charity for all; with firmness in the right, as God gives us to see the right, let us strive on to

finish the work we are in; to bind up the nation's wounds, to care for him who shall have borne the battle, and for his widow, and his orphan—to do all which may achieve and cherish a just and lasting peace among ourselves and with all nations.

Even as Lincoln spoke, the Union army was well on its way to securing the South. "Sherman had marched from Atlanta to the sea, capturing the coastal city of Savannah, then slashed his way northward through the Southern heartland. Charleston, South Carolina, where the war had started, surrendered to Union forces in February," writes Russell Freedman in *Lincoln: A Photobiography*. "By March, Sherman had invaded North Carolina and was driving toward a rendezvous with Grant's armies in Virginia."

On March 28 Lincoln met with his top commanders—Grant, Sherman, and Admiral David Dixon Porter—to discuss final plans for ending the war. All agreed the Confederacy was on the brink of surrender, yet Lincoln repeatedly inquired: "Must more blood be shed? Cannot this last bloody battle be avoided?" Peace was foremost on Lincoln's mind. As the leaders discussed how to deal with the postwar South, Lincoln made his views known. He believed that harsh treatment would only fuel anger and hatred toward the victors. "There must be no revenge, no treason trials, and no executions. Lincoln required only that the Confederates cease fighting and turn in their weapons," explains William L. Jones in *Generals in Blue and Gray*. He quotes Lincoln as saying, "Let them once surrender and reach their homes, they won't take up arms again. Let them all go, officers and all. . . . Let them have their horses to plow with. . . . I want no one punished; treat them liberally all around. We want those people to return to their allegiance to the Union and submit to the laws."

When Confederate President Jefferson Davis, along with General Lee and his troops, fled Richmond on April 2, 1865, Grant did not fire at them. Reflecting Lincoln's attitude, he said, "I had not the heart to turn the artillery upon such a mass of defeated and fleeing men." Instead of malice, Lincoln instructed his generals to show mercy. Food and medical supplies were immediately brought into Richmond, which had suffered under a long siege before it fell.

Lincoln never showed malice toward the South. Instead he urged "charity for all." He desired to see the country restored and healed. He spoke from his heart when he promised "all faithful citizens, who have been disturbed in their rights, a certain and speedy restoration." Unfortunately, he didn't live to see this occur, but his attitude toward the South set in motion a legacy of enduring unity and peace.

Today, as we reap the blessings of a nation restored, we should strive to "lay aside all malice." We should avoid harboring hard feelings toward those who oppose us and instead pray for peace and reconciliation. As you pray, ask God to soften your heart and help you love those who "spitefully use you." Lincoln often asked God for help in this area. We all need God's empowering love to "return good for evil."

> But if you love those who love you, what credit is that to you? For even sinners love those who love them. And if you do good to those who do good to you, what credit

is that to you? For even sinners do the same. And if you lend to those from whom you hope to receive back, what credit is that to you? For even sinners lend to sinners to receive as much back. But love your enemies, do good, and lend, hoping for nothing in return; and your reward will be great, and you will be sons of the Most High. For He is kind to the unthankful and evil.

Luke 6:32–35

45

BE AN ENGAGED LEADER

*I, who am not an especially brave man, have had to
sustain the sinking courage of those professional fighters in critical times.*

Abraham Lincoln

Are you an absentee manager? Do you interact with
your staff or hide in your office? Do your kids say
you're "there but not there"? All of us experience moments
when we're disengaged. But in order to be an effective boss,
employee, parent, or spouse, we must learn the importance
of engaging with those around us. As a hands-on leader,
Lincoln understood the importance of familiarizing himself

193

with the people he depended on. He was deeply occupied and absorbed in his work, especially in terms of the war effort.

In 1861 the newly invented telegraph was revolutionizing communication. It allowed correspondence to occur rapidly between distant geographic areas. Lincoln constructed a telegraph office across the street from the White House and spent a great deal of time there. In fact, during his presidency he spent more time in the telegraph office than anywhere else aside from the White House. "His tall, homely form could be seen crossing the well-shaded lawn between the White House and the War Department day after day with unvaried regularity," wrote the manager of the telegraph office.

"Lincoln could have waited in the White House for a messenger to bring him word of progress in key battles," comments Donald T. Phillips in *Lincoln on Leadership*. "But he preferred to be right there, peering over the shoulder of the decoder and getting the information as fast as it came in." Lincoln positioned himself as close as possible to the events as they unfolded. He also wanted the raw facts. "He needed to know the truth," writes Phillips. "And Abraham Lincoln had an innate ability to perceive the truth. He could receive information unbiased by filters and prejudices, process it, and then communicate it in the common man's vernacular so that everyone could understand."

Throughout the war, David Homer Bates managed the War Department telegraph. He painstakingly recorded Lincoln's daily experiences in the telegraph office from 1861 to 1865 in a five-hundred-page book entitled *Lincoln in the Telegraph*

Office. "The military telegraph was vital to the waging of the Civil War," notes Bates. "It was also vital to the distinctive and forceful manner of Lincoln's wielding his authority as commander in chief." Although many criticized Lincoln for micromanaging the military, his secretary John Hay observed admiringly that "The old man sits here and wields like a backwoods Jupiter the bolts of war and the machinery of government with a hand equally steady and equally firm."

Lincoln was the first president and commander in chief to maintain almost instant contact with armies in distant fields of war. In 1908 Senator Nathan Scott of West Virginia commented that "History records no other war where the armies were so widely scattered and where prior to ours, they were so well informed of each other's movements." Bates records that throughout the war, Lincoln sent ten or twelve dispatches to various generals daily, "almost invariably in his own handwriting, his copy being remarkably neat and legible, with seldom an erasure or correction."

Lincoln's secretaries, Nicolay and Hay, noted that "His thoughts by day and anxiety by night fed upon the intelligence which the telegraph brought. . . . It is safe to say that no general in the army studied his maps and scanned his telegrams with half the industry—and it may be added with half the intelligence—which Mr. Lincoln gave to his."

"Lincoln's habit was to go immediately to the [telegraph] drawer each time he came into our room," records Bates. He "read over the telegrams, beginning at the top, until he came to the one he had seen at his last previous visit. When this point was reached he almost always said 'Well, boys, I am down to raisins.'" When one of the cipher-operators asked what he meant, Lincoln told him the story of a little girl who ate so much on her birthday, topping it all off with raisins for dessert, that she became violently ill. "When the doctor arrived she was busy casting up her accounts. The genial doctor, scrutinizing the contents in the vessel, noticed some small black objects that had just appeared." The doctor then announced to the worried parents that all danger was past as the child was "down to raisins." So, Lincoln said, "when I reach the message in this pile which I saw on my last visit, I know that I need go no further."

Lincoln occupied the telegraph office from the very first days of the war to the last. Bates recounts that in 1861 Lincoln was in the telegraph office when he received the news of the first Union soldier to die, his young friend Colonel Elmer Ellsworth. Bates again sat on the receiving end of a dispatch sent to Lincoln on April 3, 1865, announcing Grant's capture of Petersburg and Richmond. From the beginning to the end of his national career, Lincoln was actively present.

By engaging himself in the intricacies of his enormous job, Lincoln gave everyone around him hope, courage, and an example to follow. Early on, he learned not to expect what he did not inspect. Because he engaged in the details and with the individuals involved in the details, he successfully completed his mission.

Fully engage yourself in your mission. Communicate, be hands-on, and get to know the people around you by spending quality time with them. Don't hide in your office or in front of the television. Get out with the troops, and lead the way to fulfilling your calling and vision!

> Be thou diligent to know the state of thy flocks, and look well to thy herds.
>
> Proverbs 27:23 KJV

46

BE RESPONSIBLE

But we ourselves must not decline the burden of re-
sponsibility, nor take counsel of unworthy passions.

Abraham Lincoln

*D*o you know people who are talented, smart, seemingly capable, but who never quite get their act together? They lack a certain discipline. They aren't responsible
for their behavior, and they refuse to accept responsibility
for their own lives. Some people who are amazingly talented
never succeed in life, merely because they refuse to accept
responsibility for themselves and for other people.

Each one of us must strive to be responsible. It's not enough
to learn, hope, and have dreams. We need to take responsi-

bility for ourselves and for others. It was one of the secrets to Abraham Lincoln's success. Many other people were as smart as Lincoln, but few others took as much responsibility as he did.

"How hard—oh, how more than hard—it is to die and leave one's country no better for the life of him that lived and died her child!" Lincoln confided to his partner William Herndon. Before the thought occurred to him to run for president, Lincoln voraciously read every newspaper he could find. "The world is dead to hope, deaf to its own death struggle made known by a universal cry," he lamented. "What is to be done? Is anything to be done? Who can do anything and how can it be done?" he pressed Herndon. "Did you ever think on those things?"

Abraham Lincoln bore a tremendous burden for his country. He held himself responsible for the freedom of millions of slaves, the unity and future of the nation, the safety of his soldiers, the happiness of his family, and the lives of his friends. Lincoln felt deep inner turmoil. Frustrated by the obscurity of being a country lawyer, he felt torn by the events unfolding around him. When the Kansas-Nebraska Act of 1854 threatened to permanently legitimize slavery, he felt he could no longer sit still. As early as 1856, he declared in a speech, "But we ourselves must not decline the burden of responsibility, nor take counsel of unworthy passions." One passion he found worthy was the pursuit of freedom for all people, regardless of race, and it was this passion that propelled him to the presidency.

In a speech on December 3, 1861, Lincoln explained the need for responsibility to rest on a single leader. "It has been said that one bad general is better than two good ones . . . that an army is better directed by a single mind, though inferior, than by two superior ones at variance and cross purposes with each other." Lincoln spent his first year in office unsuccessfully trying to get his cabinet members to agree with one another. "And the same is true of all joint operations wherein those engaged can have none but a common end in view and can differ only as to the choice of means."

Lincoln often referred to the war as a "tumultuous storm" and likened his administration to a gigantic ship. Not surprisingly, he expounded on this analogy in his annual address: "In a storm at sea no one on board can wish the ship to sink, and yet not infrequently all go down together because too many will direct and no single mind can be allowed to control." In other words, responsibility must be centralized. Committees cannot be held accountable to accomplish every task, because in the end, the leader is responsible and will be held accountable. And Lincoln understood that he was that person.

Lincoln was not afraid of responsibility. "I have said nothing but what I am willing to live by and if it be the pleasure of God, to die by," he told an audience in Independence Hall in 1861. He believed leadership required taking responsibility—and as a leader, he held himself accountable to God and to his country. He was driven by strength of purpose and the resolve to see his goals come to pass.

If you lack a sense of purpose, pray that God will give you a burden—something that will compel you to undertake a cause greater than your own desires. Don't hide from the concerns of others; if they neglect the greatness that resides within them, no one will benefit from the good things they are destined to share.

> Then I will appoint responsible shepherds who will care for them, and they will never be afraid again.
>
> Jeremiah 23:4 NLT

47

WAIT ON GOD'S TIMING

Let us diligently apply the means, never doubting that a just God, in His own good time, will give us the rightful result.

Abraham Lincoln

*W*e all question God's timing, especially when we're experiencing tough times. We want God to heal us now, help us now, pay our bills now, or reveal his plans for our lives right now. Although Lincoln was a patient man, he grew weary of the war. He urged the nation to hold on, to wait on God's timing, as the Civil War raged, beginning on April 12, 1861. Four bloody years later, after the South finally surrendered, the number of people who had died as the result of the war totaled 970,000—more than the number who have died in all other American wars combined.

"War, at the best, is terrible, and this war of ours, in its magnitude and its duration, is one of the most terrible," Lincoln told a Philadelphia audience on June 16, 1864. "It has deranged business. . . . It has destroyed property and ruined homes; it has produced a national debt and taxation unprecedented . . . it has carried mourning to almost every home, until it can almost be said that the Heavens are hung in black." Yet he continually exhorted his listeners to wait on God.

On October 3, 1863, in his Thanksgiving Proclamation, Lincoln acknowledged again the necessity of waiting for the divine purposes of God to unfold. "No human counsel hath devised nor hath any mortal hand worked out these great things." Six months later, Lincoln stated, "When the war began, three years ago, neither party, nor any man, expected it would last till now. . . . But here we are; the war has not ended. . . . So true it is that man proposes, but God disposes." And as the war persisted into the fall of 1864, after three and a half years of brutal losses, Lincoln made the following statement: "The purposes of the Almighty are perfect, and must prevail, though we erring mortals may fail to accurately perceive them in advance. We hoped for a happy termination of this terrible war long before this; but God knows best."

Lincoln possessed remarkable patience. Likewise we should exercise patience even when the going gets tough, acknowledging that God always has a reason behind his work. Even before being elected president, Lincoln believed that God was working out his greatest good in his perfect timing. During a trial in July of 1842 Lincoln wrote to his good friend Joshua Speed, "Whatever He designs He will do for me yet. 'Stand still, and see the salvation of the Lord!'" In July of 1864, aware that people were growing impatient and weary with the war, Lincoln urged the American people to ask the Holy Spirit to intervene. In one of many proclamations, he invited the people of the United States "to invoke the influence of the Holy Spirit to guide the counsels of the government with wisdom adequate to so great a national emergency." His thoughtful invocation continued as follows:

> To visit with tender care and consolation throughout the length and breadth of our land all those who, through the vicissitudes of marches, voyages, battles, and sieges have been brought to suffer in mind, body, or estate, and finally to lead the whole nation through the paths of repentance and submission to the Divine Will back to the perfect enjoyment of union and fraternal peace.

It was the first and only time a president of the United States referred to the Holy Spirit in a proclamation.

Lincoln continued to encourage the nation to wait on God's timing until the very end of the war. In his Second Inaugural Address, on March 4, 1865, when victory was imminent, Lincoln still boldly asserted, "If God wills that [the war] continue until all the wealth piled up by the bondsman's 250 years of unrequited toil shall be sunk, and until every drop of blood drawn with the lash shall be paid by another drawn with the sword . . . so still must it be said, 'the judgments of the Lord are true and righteous altogether.'" Regarding the issue of waiting on God's timing, Lincoln was immovable.

We can learn from Lincoln the value of waiting on God, especially when it seems as if things can get no worse. In our darkest hours we must learn to trust and wait on God. As Lincoln said to Secretary Seward in July of 1864, "The Lord has never yet deserted me, and I did not believe He would this time." Learn to wait on God's timing. You have not been deserted, nor will you ever be.

> But those who wait on the LORD
> Shall renew their strength;
> They shall mount up with wings like eagles,
> They shall run and not be weary,
> They shall walk and not faint.

Isaiah 40:31

48

TAKE TIME TO MINISTER

God, and Eternity, and Heaven were very near to me today.

Abraham Lincoln

Abraham Lincoln was more than the country's president; he was also the country's pastor. From a very early age, Lincoln's compassion called him into pastoral roles. During the Civil War, as casualties and injuries mounted, he visited hospitals and ministered to the sick and injured. For Abraham and Mary Todd Lincoln, this also helped to relieve the stress of their own daily struggles and their own grief. Facing scores of wounded soldiers who were suffering or dying and being exposed to disease and infection was certainly difficult. But often when we minister to others in desperate need, our own needs become less desperate, and we in turn are ministered to.

Both Abraham and Mary Todd visited with injured soldiers, brought fruit and flowers, wrote letters home on their behalf, and sat with people who were dying. Even before the pressing demands of his presidency, before the horrors of war, Lincoln demonstrated his compassionate bedside manner. In *The Soul of Abraham Lincoln*, William E. Barton describes a time when Lincoln's legal services were required at the home of an elderly woman who was near death. He had been summoned to prepare her last will and testament. There at her bedside, he drew up the documents and oversaw the signing and witnessing of the will.

Barton tells how the elderly woman turned to Lincoln and said, "Now I have my affairs for this world arranged satisfactorily. I am thankful to say that long before this I have made preparation for the other life I am so soon to enter." She explained that many years before she had confessed Christ as her Lord and Savior. "Your faith in Christ is wise and strong," Lincoln reassured her. "You are to be congratulated in passing through life so usefully, and into the life beyond so hopefully."

"Mr. Lincoln," she replied, "won't you read a few verses out of the Bible for me?" He was offered a Bible, but instead of taking it, he recited the twenty-third psalm, "Though I walk through the valley of the shadow of death I will fear no evil, for thou art with me; thy rod and thy staff they comfort me" (KJV). He then shared from memory the fourteenth chapter of John, "In my father's house there are many mansions; if it were not so, I would have told you. I go to prepare a place for you. And if I go to prepare a place for you, I will come again and receive you unto myself; that where I am, there ye may be also" (KJV).

"Then with a tenderness and pathos that enthralled everyone in the room," writes Barton, he recited the last stanza of "Rock of Ages":

> While I draw this fleeting breath,
> When mine eyes shall close in death,
> When I rise to worlds unknown,
> See Thee on Thy judgment throne,
> Rock of Ages, cleft for me,
> Let me hide myself in Thee.

Moments later an expression of peace lit her face, and then the woman passed away. As Lincoln rode home in silence, his traveling companion turned to him and said, "Mr. Lincoln, ever since what has just happened back there in the farmhouse, I have been thinking that it is very extraordinary that you should so perfectly have acted as pastor as well as attorney." After several moments, Lincoln replied, "God, and Eternity, and Heaven were very near to me today."

During the war, Lincoln used his pastor's heart to minister at the bedsides of injured and dying soldiers. He comforted them, listened to their experiences, and told his endless stories. Author Elizabeth Smith Brownstein writes, "Lincoln's mere appearance was enough to boost morale, but he did more than that; he would go from bed to bed with a personal word for each soldier." He did everything within his power to provide the best hospitals and care, sometimes paying out of his own pocket for special equipment to treat the peculiarities of war injuries. Both Abraham and Mary paid regular visits to makeshift military hospitals throughout the war, "sometimes together, sometimes alone," adds Brownstein.

Mary in particular took up the cause of convalescing soldiers. She raised money for greatly needed fruits and vegetables to prevent scurvy, which had resulted from patients being poorly fed. She brought fresh-cut flowers to counter the odors of disinfectant and decay. She wrote letters for the soldiers and in 1862 served Christmas dinner to the patients. "Among the ladies who visit the hospitals none is more indefatigable," wrote one observer.

In her classic 1895 biography, *The Life of Abraham Lincoln*, Ida M. Tarbell recounts one of Lincoln's last hospital visits. One week before his assassination, Lincoln visited the Army of the Potomac at City Point, Virginia. Lincoln's guide, a nineteen-year-old agent for the United States Sanitary Commission, noted his "gentleness, his friendly greetings to the sick and wounded, his quiet humor . . . and his genuine interest in the welfare of the soldiers." When Lincoln entered the wards occupied by the wounded Southern prisoners, his guide respectfully informed him, "Mr. President, you won't want to go in there; they are only rebels." Lincoln gently placed his hand on the young man's shoulder and quietly answered, "You mean Confederates."

There was nothing left for me to do after the President's remark but to go with him through these three wards; and I could not see but that he was just as kind, his hand shakings just as hearty, his interest just as real for the welfare of the men, as when he was among our own soldiers.

When I visited next day these three wards, the Southern officers and soldiers were full of praise for 'Abe' Lincoln . . . and when a week afterwards the news came of the assassination, there was no truer sorrow nor greater indignation anywhere than was shown by these same Confederates.

As busy as the president and the first lady were, they set apart time to minister to the needs of the sick and wounded soldiers. Certainly, even as busy or overburdened as we feel we are today, none of us bears the weight of overseeing a country in the midst of war while at the same time grieving the death of a child. When we are helping other people—when we are ministering God's love—it's then that we feel closest to heaven.

> Come, let us go back and again visit and help and minister to the brethren in every town where we made known the message of the Lord, and see how they are getting along.
>
> Acts 15:36 AMP

49

LIVE WITH AN ETERNAL PERSPECTIVE

In times like the present, men should utter nothing for which they would not be responsible through time and eternity.

Abraham Lincoln

S urely God would not have created such a being as man, with an ability to grasp the infinite, to exist only for a day!" Lincoln said early in his political career. "No, no, man was made for immortality!" he exclaimed to his Chicago audience in September of 1857. Even as a young lawyer in 1850, upon visiting Niagara Falls, he expressed an eternal view of the world: "When Columbus first sought this continent, when Christ suffered on the cross, when Moses led Israel through the Red Sea, nay, even when Adam first came from the hand of his Maker, then as now, Niagara was roaring here." Lincoln felt a sense of and a connection to eternity.

Well into the Civil War, when his beloved son Willie died, Lincoln began to think about his own life from an eternal perspective. The war had taken its toll, but when Willie died, he was overwhelmed with grief. Informed of the president's misery, the Rev. Francis Vinton paid him a visit. Vinton said, "Mr. President, it is natural that you should mourn for your son—one whom you so tenderly loved." Vinton then exhorted the president:

> But is it not your duty to rise above the affliction? Your duties are to the living. They are far greater than those of a father to his son. You are at the head of the nation—a father of the people; and are you not unfitting yourself for a right exercise of the responsibility that God has laid upon you?

Early Lincoln biographer and journalist C. C. Coffin recorded this conversation in his 1893 *Life of Abraham Lincoln*. He describes how the Rev. Vinton gently encouraged Lincoln from a biblical perspective, "You ought not to mourn for your son as lost—that is not Christianity, but heathenism." Lincoln listened carefully as Vinton spoke, "Your son is above. Do you not remember that passage in the Gospels: God 'is not the God of the dead, but the God of the living'?" (Mark 12:27 KJV).

To this Lincoln replied, "Alive? Alive? Do you say that Willie is alive? Pray do not mock me." But the reverend assured him, "Yes, Mr. Lincoln, alive. Jesus Christ has said it." After a few thoughtful moments, Lincoln looked up with tears rolling down his cheeks and firmly grasped hold of the clergyman. "Alive! Alive!" he exclaimed. "Yes, Mr. Lincoln," Vinton reassured him, "it is one of God's most precious truths."

Reverend Vinton offered to send Lincoln a sermon he had preached on the subject, which Lincoln gratefully accepted. When the sermon arrived, writes Coffin, "Mr. Lincoln was so impressed by its treatment of the Resurrection and Immortality that he read it again and again, and caused it to be copied. . . . The thought that in the radiant he would once more clasp his boy in his arms made his sorrow easier to bear than ever before." From that time forward, Lincoln was able to fully return to the pressing affairs of the nation.

It appears that from this point forward, Lincoln viewed the war, the nation, and his own life from an eternal perspective. The way he evaluated decisions, events, and actions began to change. He had already professed faith in God and had read his Bible, but he gained a fresh understanding of eternity. It emboldened him and strengthened his faith in God and in his work. He later confided that he didn't think he'd live to see the end of the war, but that he'd see it from a "long distance." When his old friend Father Charles Chiniquy came to visit him from Springfield to warn him of the many assassination plans that he had heard circulating, Lincoln picked up his Bible and read out loud Deuteronomy 3:25–27: "I pray thee, let me go over, and see the good land that is beyond Jordan. . . . But the LORD was wroth with me for your sakes, and would not hear me: and the LORD said unto me . . . thou shalt not go over this Jordan" (KJV). And then he solemnly said:

Do you know that I hear in my soul, as the voice of God, giving me the rebuke which was given to Moses? There is a still, but solemn voice which tells me that I will see those things only from a long distance, and that I will be among the dead, when the nation, which God granted me to lead through those awful trials, will cross the Jordan, and dwell in that Land of Promise. . . . It seems to me that the Lord wants today, as He wanted in the days of Moses, another victim—a victim which He had himself chosen, anointed, and prepared for the sacrifice, by raising it above the rest of the people. I cannot conceal from you that my impression is that I am the victim. . . . But just as the Lord heard no murmur from the lips of Moses when He told him that he had to die before crossing the Jordan for the sins of his people, so I hope and pray that He will hear no murmur from me when I fall for my nation's sake.

Deeply moved, the two knelt down to pray before Father Chiniquy departed. Perhaps to encourage his friend, or maybe himself, Lincoln concluded, "Now would it not be the greatest of honors and privileges bestowed upon me, if God in His infinite love, mercy, and wisdom would put me between His faithful servant, Moses, and His eternal Son, Jesus, that I might die as they did, for my nation's sake?"

We are reminded of the bigger picture and greater plan that God has ordained for the greatest good of all. The hope that we have in Christ is beyond what we could dare to ask or imagine; remembering this, we too can stand in the gap and live sacrificially as Lincoln did. Don't be anxious about the circumstances you find yourself in today—live with an eternal perspective. When things don't go well and it seems your world is falling apart, remember that God has always been in charge and he always will be.

> Let them do good, that they be rich in good works, ready to give, willing to share, storing up for themselves a good foundation for the time to come, that they may lay hold on eternal life.
>
> 1 Timothy 6:18–19

50

Be an Evangelist

It is ungodly; it is ungodly; no doubt it is ungodly!

Abraham Lincoln

Do you want to be a world changer? At some point in our lives, each of us has the desire to transform our world. We want to stop a war, end poverty, rectify a particular injustice, or usher in a new political order. And, of course, we also want to spread the gospel and save souls—and do it in a manner similar to Paul, Martin Luther, or Billy Graham. Then someone comes along who transforms the way we live, and we scratch our heads and wonder, *How did he do that?*

Abraham Lincoln understood what it means to change the world. He was an evangelist for the cause of freedom. He left us with a biblical blueprint for how to carry out a great commission.

If you look up *evangelism* in Webster's dictionary, it says, "Any zealous effort in propagandizing for a cause." But Guy Kawasaki, author of *Selling the Dream*, says that evangelism is more than merely a zealous effort; rather, it is "the process of convincing people to believe in your product or idea as much as you do." Real evangelism leads to permanent change, and it has a snowball effect. It changes how people think and behave, not just today, but far into the future. That was the kind of evangelism Lincoln practiced.

On November 19, 1839, at the Second Presbyterian Church in Springfield, Illinois, Lincoln began to grasp what it meant to be an agent of social transformation. He joined an impromptu debate between Whigs and Democrats—one of his first forays into politics. He debated with great finesse and was urged to join a local campaign. Lincoln held a deep-seated desire to change the world, and now he saw an opportunity to do it.

Lincoln campaigned with great fervor. It energized him and, according to Albert Bledsoe, it made him "most merry." He crisscrossed the state on horseback, speaking with farmers in their fields and in their taverns. He gave speeches whenever and wherever anybody would listen. "We must fight the devil with fire," he exclaimed. "We must defeat the Democrats, or the country will be ruined."

Lincoln lost his first election, but he stumped around Illinois for the next twenty years. He became an evangelist, not merely a politician. He persuaded people to believe in the cause of freedom, not in Abraham Lincoln. And he was relentless.

His law partner William Herndon said he was "like a sleeping lion . . . a little engine that knew no rest." Provoked and always engaged, Lincoln could not get his mind off slavery. John C. Waugh writes in *One Man Great Enough* that Lincoln's zeal was as "fervent, emotional, and raucous as a religious camp meeting."

Not only did Lincoln speak, but he also wrote incessantly. Lincoln wrote campaign circulars and intended to "organize the whole State." He sent letters to friends and foes. He studied history and law books and always looked for opportunities to debate colleagues. He organized precincts and counties on behalf of his party. He rallied the faithful. "The fight must go on," he'd say after each loss.

Even after a crushing loss to Stephen Douglas for the United States Senate, Lincoln pressed on with enthusiasm. He exported his message to Wisconsin, Indiana, and Ohio, giving dozens of speeches. Waugh writes that he "delivered his gospel vigorously." Observers said his oration reminded them of "the sweep of a great elm." Soon he received invitations to speak in places as far away as Boston and New York. He hounded Douglas, following him around the country in opposition to slavery. Lincoln made some 175 major speeches outside of Illinois.

Lincoln's short discourse in 1839 started an avalanche. By August of 1859 throngs of young people marched through city streets, beating drums and chanting Lincoln's name. "Old Abe Lincoln came out of the wilderness," they sang. Townspeople displayed symbols from Lincoln's past, and the rallies grew larger than America had ever known.

By August of 1860 when Lincoln was nominated for president of the United States by the newly formed Republican Party, he was no longer a voice in the wilderness. Supporters swarmed Springfield—up to 70,000 of them on August 15, 1860. "The enthusiasm was beyond all bounds . . . I never saw so dense and large a crowd," wrote a reporter for the *Cincinnati Gazette*.

Abraham Lincoln spread the good news of freedom with fervor, sincere commitment, and perseverance. He didn't run campaigns; his life was a campaign.

> Keep your head in all situations, endure hardship, do the work of an evangelist, discharge all the duties of your ministry.
>
> 2 Timothy 4:5 NIV

Sources Cited

Barton, William E. *The Soul of Abraham Lincoln*. Chicago: University of Illinois Press, 2005.

Brownstein, Elizabeth S. *Lincoln's Other White House*. Hoboken, NJ: John Wiley & Sons, 2005.

Carpenter, Francis B. *Six Months at the White House*. New York: Hurd and Houton, 1866.

Carwardine, Richard. *Lincoln: A Life of Purpose and Power*. New York: Alfred A. Knopf, 2006.

Cox, Hank H. *Lincoln and the Sioux Uprising of 1862*. Nashville: Cumberland House, 2005.

Donald, David H. *Lincoln*. New York: Simon & Schuster, 1995.

Fox, George G. *Abraham Lincoln's Religion*. New York: Exposition Press, 1959.

Goodwin, Doris K. *Team of Rivals*. New York: Simon & Schuster, 2005.

Guelzo, Allen C. *Abraham Lincoln: Redeemer President*. Grand Rapids: Eerdmans, 2003.

Herndon, William H. *Herndon's Lincoln: A True Story of a Great Life*. Springfield, IL: The Herndon's Lincoln Publishing Company, 1888.

Hill, John W. *Abraham Lincoln: Man of God*. New York: G. P. Putnam's Sons, 1920.

Holzer, Harold. *Lincoln at Cooper Union*. New York: Simon & Schuster, 2004.

Horner, Harlan H. *The Growth of Lincoln's Faith*. New York: Abingdon Press, 1939.

Jayne, Allen. *Lincoln and the American Manifesto*. New York: Prometheus, 2007.

Jones, Edgar D. *Lincoln and the Preachers*. New York: Harper & Brothers, 1948.

Lind, Michael. *What Lincoln Believed*. New York: Anchor Books, 2004.

Macartney, Clarence E. *Lincoln and the Bible*. Nashville: Abingdon-Cokesbury.

McClure, J. B. *Anecdotes and Stories of Abraham Lincoln*. Mechanicsburg, PA: Stackpole Books, 2006.

Miller, William L. *Lincoln's Virtues*. New York: Vintage Books, 2002.

McPherson, James M. *Abraham Lincoln and the Second American Revolution*. New York: Oxford University Press, 1991.

Nicolay, Helen. *Personal Traits of Abraham Lincoln*. Mechanicsburg, PA: Stackpole Books, 2006.

Shaw, Archer H. *The Lincoln Encyclopedia*. New York: Macmillan, 1950.

Shenk, Joshua W. *Lincoln's Melancholy*. New York: Mariner Books, 2005.

Smith, Gary S. *Faith and the Presidency: From George Washington to George W. Bush*. New York: Oxford University Press, 2006.

Tarbell, Ida M. *The Life of Abraham Lincoln*. New York: The Lincoln Historical Society, 1902.

Thomas, Benjamin P. *"Lincoln's Humor" and Other Essays*. Chicago: University of Illinois Press, 2002.

Waugh, John C. *One Man Great Enough: Abraham Lincoln's Road to the Civil War*. Orlando: Harcourt, 2007.

Whipple, Wayne. *The Story-Life of Lincoln*. Philadelphia: The John C. Winston Company, 1908.

White, Ronald C. *Lincoln's Greatest Speech*. New York: Simon & Schuster, 2002.

Wills, Garry. *Under God*. New York: Simon & Schuster, 1990.

Wilson, Douglas L. *Honor's Voice: The Transformation of Abraham Lincoln*. New York: Alfred A. Knopf, 1998.

Wolf, William J. *The Almost Chosen People*. New York: Doubleday & Company, 1959.

Thomas Freiling is the author and editor of a historical anthology called *Reagan's God and Country* and of the daily prayer devotional, *Prayers to Move Your Mountains*. He served on the staff of the U.S. House of Representatives and also was publisher of Creation House books in Orlando, Florida. Freiling is currently president of Xulon Press in Vienna, Virginia.